北大培文杯
全国青少年英语创意写作大赛优秀作品

写给未来的自己 第②季

刁克利　高秀芹　主编

TOMORROW
COMES
TODAY

中国人民大学出版社
·北 京·

大赛评委会

主　席

颜海平　　　　　　　清华大学外国语言文学系主任、教授

D. 麦克尔·林赛　　　美国高登大学校长
（D. Michael Lindsay）

评　委

大卫·达姆罗什　　　美国哈佛大学比较文学系教授
（David Damrosch）

布鲁斯·罗宾斯　　　美国哥伦比亚大学英语系教授
（Bruce Robbins）

蒂莫西·穆雷　　　　美国康奈尔大学人文研究所所长、教授
(Timothy Murray)

艾米·维拉睿鹤　　　美国康奈尔大学电影系主任、教授
(Amy Villarejo)

大卫·古登堡　　　　美国加州大学人文研究所主任教授
(David Goldberg)

约翰·布莱尔　　　　瑞士日内瓦大学教授
(John Blair)

柏右铭　　　　　　　美国华盛顿大学电影系教授
(Yomi Braester)

李　尧	北京外国语大学教授
石　坚	四川大学外国语学院教授
张绍杰	东北师范大学教授
虞建华	上海外国语大学语言文学研究所所长、教授
王顺珠	美国瑞德大学教授
程朝翔	北京大学外国语学院教授
高峰枫	北京大学外国语学院教授
黄必康	北京大学外国语学院教授
刘建华	北京大学外国语学院教授
赵白生	北京大学世界文学研究所所长、教授
康士林 (Nicholas Koss)	北京大学中文系特聘教授
张　沛	北京大学比较文学与比较文化研究所副教授
秦立彦	北京大学比较文学与比较文化研究所副教授
张文霞	清华大学外国语言文学系书记、教授
曹　莉	清华大学外国语言文学系副主任、教授
封宗信	清华大学外国语言文学系教授
王敬慧	清华大学外国语言文学系教授
程晓堂	北京师范大学外国语言文学学院教授
金　莉	北京外国语大学英语学院教授、《外国文学》主编
张　剑	北京外国语大学英语学院院长、教授
郭棲庆	北京外国语大学英语学院教授
马海良	北京外国语大学教授
宁一中	北京语言大学外国文学与文化研究所所长、教授

沈建青	北京语言大学人文学院教授
王　炎	北京外国语大学教授
郭继德	山东大学外国语学院教授
陈世丹	中国人民大学外国语学院教授
刁克利	中国人民大学外国语学院教授
尹文涓	首都师范大学比较文学系教授
曲卫国	复旦大学外国语言文学学院院长、教授
谈　峥	复旦大学外国文学研究所所长、教授
杨乃乔	复旦大学教授
王柏华	复旦大学教授
李尚宏	上海外国语大学英语系教授
金衡山	华东师范大学外语学院副院长、教授
朱　刚	南京大学外国语学院院长、教授，全国美国文学研究会会长
杨金才	南京大学外国语学院副院长、教授
徐　昉	南京大学外国语学院教授、写作专家
何莲珍	浙江大学外国语言文化与国际交流学院院长、教授
胡开宝	上海交通大学外国语学院院长、教授
郭英剑	中央民族大学外国语学院院长、教授
高建平	中国社会科学院研究员
黄　梅	中国社会科学院研究员
刘　岩	广东外语外贸大学教授
文　旭	西南大学外国语学院院长、教授
孙　博	加拿大网络电视台台长
张箭飞	武汉大学教授、《长江学术》副主编

蔡小容	武汉大学外国语言文学学院教授
聂珍钊	华中师范大学教授、《外国文学研究》主编
苏　晖	华中师范大学教授、《外国文学研究》副主编
谢　娜	北京大学出版社海外合作部主任
赵　欣	北京大学出版社海外合作部编辑
黄瑞明	北京大学出版社外语编辑部主任助理、副编审
李　颖	北京大学出版社外语编辑部编辑

文学是生命的延展

刁克利

在每个人的成长过程中，文学任重而道远。《周易·象传》有云："山下出泉，蒙。君子以果行育德。"文学能够启迪心志，带给人心灵上的启蒙。从文学中，我们可以读出不断丰富和充盈的人生。在文学感受和文学造诣上的每一层进阶，都代表着自己的成长。我们对文学的理解也随着经验的积累日渐加深，这里的经验既包括人生阅历，也包括阅读经历。几千年来，古今中外的经典读物汗牛充栋，这些都是我们可以汲取的宝贵财富。

在文以化人、文以育德的同时，文学还可以陶冶性情，有其娱乐性特征。早在古罗马时期，贺拉斯就提出"寓教于乐"。文学可以让人们获得自然的灵感，得到身心的愉悦。在文学写作中，用文字张扬个性的过程，也是一个感知自我的过程。在文学阅读中，我们可以发掘文字之美，发现文学带来的独特感动，收获对生命的崇敬热爱。

在一个国家或民族的成长过程中，文学同样肩负着重大使命。人类巴别塔的重构，不仅仅需要跨越语言的鸿沟，还需要消弭不同民族文化思想的隔阂。不同民族之间，文学作品的传承与交流碰撞，使得不同民族的文学能够相互理解和沟通，更进一步地促进人类文明的发展。

近年来创意写作方兴未艾，许多学校都建立起创意写作中心。一年一度的创意写作国际论坛和世界华人创意写作大会持续举行，使"作家可以培养，写作人人可为"的观念蔚然成风。在这样一个大众写作的时代，写作日趋生活化，每个人都想要表达自己，想要去讲故事，但并不是每个人都能把故事讲好。文学来源于生活，又高于生活，如何在平淡日常中提炼素材，是创意写作教学的重点所在。

"北大培文杯"创意写作活动是创意写作理念的一次成功实践。参加"北大培文杯"的青少年们，思维能力和创造能力都得到了极大的提升，他们带着文学热忱，勇于书写自我，自信地在文章中展现出朝气蓬勃的青春面貌。与此同时，英文的创意写作帮助青少年培育世界眼光，鼓励青少年走出国门，进入更广阔的天地。

在当今时代，创意写作作品集是十分必要的，特别是像《写给未来的自己》这样的英文的创意写作作品集。《写给未来的自己》全书共四部分，归集了科幻作品、童话故事、青春风采、社会题裁四个类别的作品。

用不同的民族语言来进行创意写作，这本身就是一种创新和挑战，它体现的是青少年精神生命的成长和敢于创新、打破陈规的力量。

希望所有的中国青少年，都能参加"北大培文杯"英文创意写作活动，利用这个优秀的平台，发挥自己的创意，挥洒自己的青春！

CONTENTS

1. Dear Mr. Robot-I 001

The Last Ten Years	吴艾婧	003
Immortal Company	王佳漪	011
Five Seconds to the Universal Century	赵　炜	020
Dear Mr. Robot-I	徐仪筱	024
Indestructible Heart	肖易佳	030
Hope	董觉非	037
The Right and the Left	姚东妮	043
Back to Zero	谭力珲	047
Ten Young Hearts of Rising Sun	武阅海	052
The Firm Wall of MORA	姚文瑾	060
Lost with the Island	赵君彤	065
Alice in April	孙菡治	069

2. Do You Hear Me, Little Prince? 075

Do You Hear Me, Little Prince?	宋元煦	077
The Golden Bells	李松晓	081
Don't Be Close to It	邱渝茜	090
Who Are You?	刘雪晗	094
The Yard Besieged	熊勉之	098
Who Is the Monster?	曾　曼	102

Don't Lose Your Label	刘佳淇	105
A Label of Status	李正锴	109
Free from Labels	吴一婕	113
To the Skyline	李松晓	117
The Label of Love	王逸菲	122
Cage of Desire	盖雪琪	126

3. Get Rid of the Label "Kid" 131

Metamorphosis	吴一凡	133
Get Rid of the Label "Kid"	陈 渔	141
The Illness	李森然	146
Tom's Adventure for Keys	周星宇	149
The Rule	王京菁	153
It Happens	车子涵	161
Vicissitudes	黄 航	166
Back	杨寒琦	170
The Locked Doors	刘沛松	174
Chase with the Tide	王 鼎	179
New Me	卓思岑	186
Under My Skin	陈佳怡	189

4. It Is Time to Connect 197

E-key Arrived—AD Script of An Online Share Car Company	李宇峰	199
The Wall of Conscience Has Been Broken down	吴希言	202
It Is Time to Connect	潘 岩	206
Walls between People	张雨菡	210
Rising Tide	张静仪	214
The Only Survivor	郭奕萱	220
People and Label	滕子牧	225
Do Labels Work?	柯思云	229

Countdown …………………………………	刘笑语	234
Ten Counts …………………………………	桂嘉雨	238
Welcome to the New Age ……………………	周雨旸	245
The Track of History ………………………	李雅婕	249

附 录 ……………………………………………… **254**

2016年"北大培文杯"英语创意写作大赛题目 …………… 254

2017年"北大培文杯"英语创意写作大赛题目 …………… 254

2018年"北大培文杯"英语创意写作大赛题目 …………… 255

DEAR MR. ROBOT-I

> ▼ The crisis of today is the joke of tomorrow.
> ——H. G. Wells

奇迹是果，幻想是根。从《弗兰肯斯坦》到儒勒·凡尔纳，从阿西莫夫到《安德的游戏》，想象之外，好的科幻文学离不开前瞻思考和危机意识，也一定离不开人性之维。

本篇所选的科幻文章异彩纷呈。小作者们在有限的篇幅内，展开了富有奇幻色彩的想象，既符合严密的科学逻辑，也展示出对于人类的思考。有的文章带着波谲云诡的悬疑底色，扣人心弦。有的文章书写人类的脉脉亲情，却又在结尾处惊天逆转。有的文章将科幻色彩融入历史，展开对理想王国的探讨。有的文章将主人公设定为智能机器人。有的文章展开了与平行时空的对话……

当科幻与时代、科幻与历史结合起来时，就会产生一种虚构空间与真实空间相结合的宏大力量。让我们在惊叹种种神奇想象之余，跟随这些文章的作者一起去探索科学的意义，感受人性的温度。

> **作者的话**
>
> 21世纪开启了人工智能的时代。在科研人员突破重重壁垒之前，亟待解决的，早已由技术难题变为伦理、哲学命题。我们至今似乎仍然谜一样地盲信着图灵测试、机器人三定律。
>
> 我们需要人工智能拥有强大的学习能力以服务人类，但同时人类对人工智能高度发达的担忧也成了"房间里的大象"：当我们的创造物产生了人性时，我们该如何判断自己存在的正当性？当大数据成为判断准则时，人类独有的"感官"存在还有多少意义？……
>
> 上帝曾为了阻止人类近神的举动，创造出不同语言阻断交流，而当这些已然不足以成为人工智能的阻碍时，通天的新巴别塔是否即将建起？

THE LAST TEN YEARS

吴艾婧

This is a report from Company X's investigator. I was asked to find some details about a survey done by our researchers. And I found a book, looking like a diary. WALL-E was on the cover with his classic line: "I don't want to survive, I want to live."

The things down here are parts of the copy of the diary.

Ten Years Before

Sunny day.

I woke up in my apartment with some bright sunlight shining towards my face. What a nice day! I got up and had a shower. The time I sat down at the dinner table, I suddenly recognized that it was already July 12th, 2030. What was special that day? Well, I was going to have a roommate. It was such a difficult thing to afford the rent of this whole apartment on my own salary, so I put an advertisement to get a roommate several months ago, and finally, a man called.

"I do hope that he would be a nice person." I was wondering when somebody knocked at the door. I stood up and opened the door gently. The man was right outside, with all of his… "Excuse me, mister, but what are they? Where is your luggage?" "Sorry to surprise you, but this is my luggage." He said with a smile on his face, "Pretty, huh? You know, I do love all my computers."

Yes, there were, in my own thought, hundreds and thousands of technical things in front of my door. I had to help him to carry all of them into the apartment, and it was such a "happy" thing to realize that I didn't even have place to put my feet.

"As I told you, I am something of an artist, which means that I need the room to be quiet and clean. You can make your 'sweet computers' stay clean, right?" "Of course, sir. By the way, you can call me Tony." He stretched his hand. "Steve." We shook hands.

The sun was still shining brightly in the blue sky, but after seeing such a mess, I couldn't be as excited as before. "We will definitely not have a good time together." I thought.

Nine Years Before

"Tony? Tony!" I knocked at the door heavily. He didn't show up for two days, and the tinker sound never stopped. How did he make that?

"Yes?"

Thank God, he was still alive.

"I know that you love your high-technique 'toys', but at least you need to have some food and some sleep."

He opened his door and came out unwillingly. "Okay, MOM. Remember I am not a teenager now?"

I cooked some food for him and after dining, pushed him into his bed. When I went out of the room, I couldn't help looking around. There was no doubt that Tony was a fantastic scientist, but suddenly, a thought came into my mind. How could he be so healthy as he had so much bad habits of daily life? Nobody can manage that except… he was a robot. This might be a ridiculous thing ten years ago, but for now, Artificial Intelligence was EVERYWHERE. An actor even announced that his soulmate was his own AI Robot. And a science company had just invented their robot for testing a few years ago. Tony worked in a science company and he didn't tend to tell me the name of it. In this case, I had some evidence to suspect that he was a robot himself.

"Did I just think about my roommate being a robot?" I was shocked by my own inference. "You are an artist, not a robot specialist. Stop your stupid imagination." I shook my head and started my work again.

Eight Years Before

"Stevie! Come here! I'd like to show you something!"

After two years spending together, we became good friends. Strange, but it was real.

I walked into his room and was scared to death. A huge, flying virtual snake came towards me. I rushed out and heavily closed my door with a "BANG". I could hear Tony burst out into laughter, so I flapped on the shut door angrily and shouted: "Oh! Tony! I have told you not to scare me with those things!"

"Come on, old man! Don't be so serious! You are in your twenties, not nineties!"

"This is the last time! I swear I will kick you out if there is another one!"

I knew I couldn't feel angry at all if I saw his face. His eyes were certainly full of joy, like twinkle stars blinking right in front of you. Nobody could be angry with such a delightful face. NOBODY.

During a year of searching and observing, I thought that I could confirm that he was a robot. Yes, I didn't drop that silly guess. Instead, it became more and more clear as time flew by. He didn't have any friends except for his scientific buddies. He didn't like to eat fruits and vegetables and loved to eat those made of oil and flour. He was a genius in computer but a disabled in daily life… How could he not be a robot? But the thought would not upset me anymore. That didn't matter whether he was a robot or a human. I liked to stay and talk with him, and for the most important part, he was my only friend till then. It really worried me to talk with other people, so it made him mean even more.

Seven Years Before

It was a rainy day with clouds floating in the sky. I hated rainy days. They were so disappointing and made me feel really bad.

I was using my pencil to scratch the paper for abreaction. Then a hand was put on my shoulder and a cup of hot chocolate was offered.

"Hey, big guy. Why do you have such a bad mood now?"

It was Tony, of course.

I didn't want to say, because I didn't want to make the people around me feel bad. So, I decided to refuse his kindness. But when I was looking up, I saw his eyes, filled with care and worries. I could tell that they were saying: "Don't be so sad. Don't do that to yourself. Would you like to talk to me? I will always be supportive to you. I will always be on your side."

Strangely, I opened my mouth and the things in my mind just slipped out like a stream. Tony sat beside me, and his eyes were gazing on me. "…and I woke up in a rainy day, my parents had all gone. I yelled and yelled, but nobody answered. After that, a few days maybe, until now, I couldn't remember my childhood clearly. I was like a man drowning in the sea— I didn't know where to go, so I came here and did some painting for living."

For the first time in my life, I opened the door of my heart to let somebody in. Tony was a good listener, he was just looking at me in a comforting way without a word, and when I finished, he hugged me and told me: "Everything will be fine, there are always hope in our life."

The rain stopped, and a rainbow showed in the sky. The world became clear again, and my world was lit up.

Six Years Before

Tony and I were preparing for a holiday to relax. As he didn't know anything about packing luggage— thinking back of what I saw for the first time he came—I did all the packing. When I went into his room for his clothes, I found that a computer was working and there was an email unread. With curiosity, I opened it up and saw the things that I would never want to know.

Dear Tony,

As for your reports so far, the company was sure that Steve-Robot No. 616 was a successful model of our further design. Also, as you mentioned before, he had already been so intelligent that he had created his own feelings, which was an unexcepted but good thing to know. Come to the office next month, and we will talk about this that time.

Company X

I felt that my body was so heavy that I couldn't even manage to stand. I fell onto the ground with my hands shaking badly. I was a robot, how could that be? I hit myself with my own fist, wanting to wake up from this horrible dream. It was hurt and nothing changed. Then I finally realized that I couldn't ever wake up. This was not a dream. I was part of a machine. I was not a human being. My face, my body, were all made up living in a system. I couldn't stop the tears running down my cheek. The world became blank again.

"Steve? What's wrong?" Tony ran inside and saw the email. His face looked pale.

"Is that real?" I asked, using up all the rest of my energy to ensure.

"Yes." He approached to give me a hug, "I'm sorry, Steve." His eyes were full of sadness.

I shook off his arms and rushed outside, but I didn't know where to go. That was it. That was why I couldn't remember my childhood. I didn't even have one. I wanted to cry but I didn't know what to cry for. I wasn't supposed to have feelings, just like the other machines. I walked along the bank of the river, where Tony found me in the evening.

"Go home." He said, his beautiful eyes were filled with tears, "Whatever you are, I am your friend, you know that, right? Come with me, trust me as you did before, I will help you. You are not just a robot, you have feelings, you are a miracle."

Now

It is already five years after that, and I am still alive, maybe it is more specific to say that I am still working. I have lived with Tony as usual for these years.

Yesterday, Tony told me that I would be shut down for a month to let him renew my brain so that I could study some functions to help him with his work. As it will happen in this week, I think it is a good thing to write my ten-year life down. I am afraid that I may forget them.

I believe in Tony heartily, and we always have faith in each other. We share our happiness and sadness, good moods and bad moods. That must be how friends are in my mind.

Hope that I could see him the minute I wake up again. I am sure I will miss him.

Do you still remember the title? Why is "the last"?

As far as I know, after that "surgery", Tony never mentioned the name "Steve" again. And the model made after Steve was published by Company X in a short time. It might just because that Steve had finished his job—which he was made for.

Did Steve wake up? I guess not.

Does Tony miss him? Maybe.

Is all worthy? No specific answer.

At last, I want to end this report with this.

Spielberg did some share through his AI:

It isn't just a question of creating a robot that can love. Isn't the real conundrum, can you get a human to love them back?

（作者学校：北京市第十二中学）
本文为2017年"北大培文杯"决赛参赛文

> **作者的话**
>
> 　　心有一隅者，庸人常自扰，无事不操劳；心系家国者，唯愿天下乂安，却不免忧国忧民，进退成愁；心怀宇宙者，虽有如山之恨、似海之愁，亦不过浩渺宇宙一蜉蝣，弹指刹那云消散，红尘喜怒皆抛闪。
>
> 　　为童，我愿心有一隅，草木风雪皆有感，一枝红梅乱心头；为人，我愿心系天下，庙堂江湖皆不计，天下苍生系胸怀；为媪，我愿心怀宇宙，万物运行自有灵，无事无物挂心间。年岁渐长，见闻日增；胸怀有变，文亦不同。此行路上，只盼一思一感皆有录，一纸一笔伴身边。
>
> 　　我以我笔写我心，我以我字释我情。漫漫长路，有笔随行。列位看官看罢，亦不过他人生中走一回，掩卷合扇，拢袖长叹，各自奔行。

IMMORTAL COMPANY

王佳漪

I

As the very first beam of sunlight leaking by the curtain and sprinkling brilliance on Verna's bed, she stretched a little bit and yawned. She walked to the front door: dad had been up since dawn, mowing and shaping the lawn, until the rosettes and lilies seemed to shine. What Verna liked the most about their garden were those lovely lilies: big pink flowers, wide open, radiant, almost frightening alive on their stems.

"I'm leaving, Mom!" After breakfast she yelled.

"Sure! Be careful on the street!" answered Mrs. White.

The teacher had said before that their primary school would take them to the movie. So this day, without school assignments and pressure, Verna found everything lovely. The weather was perfect, windless, and warm. Only the blue was veiled with light gold, as it was sometimes in early summer. And how adorable were those orange trees! They had their broad, gleaming leaves and clusters of yellow fruit lifted up to the sun, proud, solitary, showing off in a kind of silent splendor. Toward her came Ashley, whom Verna had always been considering as her best friend forever. Ashley was in her black hat adorned with golden daisies, and a long red velvet ribbon was swinging by her cheek.

"What an elegant girl I'm coming to!" Verna approved. She joined her hands with Ashley as they heading for the school.

II

The movie was quite scary, and they were all silent while walking out from the theatre.

"Cheer up, Verna, I mean··· do you really believe it, that you will die if you count backward?"

"Shut up, Adam, that's frightening!" Replied a timid girl.

"Ten, nine, eight, seven, six··· have you died? Ha-ha-ha···"

Boys left them, laughing aloud. But Ashley suddenly clapped her hands to her ears.

"Don't count!" She yelled.

"What happened, Ashley?" Asked Verna in a caring voice.

"Never mind."

Hardly had Verna gotten home when she began to recall the plots in the movie. It was said that in a certain kind of occasion, one would die if he counted back from ten to one. She took a deep breath, stretched and let them out.

"Uh!" she sighed.

As she decided to let it go, the phone rang.

"It's me, Ashley," Ashley's voice trembled, "I··· I want to tell you something."

"What's wrong?"

"I mean··· I heard it, just when they were counting backwards, from ten to one. It was a strange sound, a sound I've never heard before. Verna, will I die?" Verna wasn't sure actually, but she said, "no dear, you won't die. It's just a story···"

She was about to continue when she heard Ashley, from the other end of the connection, counting.

"Ten, nine, eight, seven, six···" The phone was hung off.

III

"It's unfortunate that our classmate, Ashely, is going to transfer to another school." Said the teacher. Verna looked at Ashley's empty chair. What happened to her? She counted backward last night. Verna was scared by her imagination, but she couldn't help thinking of Ashley.

After school, Verna went to Ashley's house, but no one answered the door. It was growing dusky, and a shadow, crab-like, moved across the window. She abruptly noticed that there was a long velvet ribbon at the front gate, the one used to be on Ashley's hat.

What she didn't see, though, was that down in the hollow, a man in black was staring at her.

When Verna came back home, she locked herself in her bedroom. The light in her room was feeble, which made her feel even creepier. "Ten." she started.

"Ten, nine, eight, seven, six, five, four, three, two, one." She counted. "Cluck!" She heard. "Ah!!" The house was filled with Verna's screaming.

"What happened, darling?" Mom and dad knocked the door and entered her room. They saw her face, full of fear, with swollen eyes and lips.

"Mom, will I die?" She stammered.

Mom and dad looked at each other and laughed, as if hearing the most ridiculous joke being told.

"You won't die, sweetie. You will live longer than both of us."

Mom said.

"Go and take a shower now. You probably need more sleep." Dad said.

By the time Verna went to bed, she was still feeling uneasy.

IV

"Knock knock!" Mr. and Mrs. White opened the door.

It was the man in black that entered the house. "Where's your daughter?"

"She's sleeping, upstairs in her room." Replied Mr. White, in a quiet tone.

The black man went upstairs to Verna's room. There, he took out his tool-bag, put on a pair of accurate glasses for repairing equipment, and started fixing. He first took off Verna's face, as if taking off a mask. What's behind the mask was astonishing: delicate small components, all connected to each other, lain orderly in Verna's brain— or "computer" might be considered more suitable here. He carefully checked every part of Verna's "computer", caught quite a lot of mistakes, and fixed them all. By the time he finished, it was midnight already.

"It is just that many mistakes have accumulated in your daughter's computer that the robot couldn't stand, and I have already fixed them all. Her life-expectancy has been prolonged by me to 20 years, so as long as she doesn't count backward, you don't have to worry about her. Her mask was a little bit loose as well, so she might have heard a weird 'cluck' sound, but I have already fastened her mask. Oh, by the by, there was a robot broken just a few days ago in that house," the black man pointed, "your daughter might be frightened, so I adjusted her memories to cheer her up."

Mr. and Mrs. White appreciated him and paid him. As the black man left their house, they kissed good night and went back to their bedroom.

V

"I'm leaving!" yelled Verna, in a happy voice.

"Sure, be careful!" replied dad.

Verna was on her way to school, and she felt everything adorable. There were two spots of sun, one on the dew, the other on the top of lavender, playing chase. They were warm and cute, like silver little stars. Verna bent down, pinched a sprig of lavender, put her thumb and forefinger to her nose and snuffed up the smell. Boys on the playground were counting backwards: "four, three, two, one!"

"Goal!" It's always hard for soccer boys to calm down.

Verna had a satisfied smile on her face: she smelt the scent of summer!

VI

Back in Verna's house.

Mr. and Mrs. White were having breakfast.

"It is good that Verna will be with us for another 20 years." said

Mr. White.

"Yeah, I don't want a new one, actually."

"Do you want to take a trip this summer vacation?" asked Mr. White.

"Do you want to take a trip this summer?"

"Take a trip this summer…"

"Ten, nine, eight, seven, six, five, four, three, two, one." A flicker of light burst out from Mr. White's ear. His eyes suddenly darkened, and his spoon slipped to the floor.

"That's what I dislike about the old version!" sighed by Mrs. White.

She switched on the TV, where news was reported.

"As is commonly known, the birth rate of human has always been lower than 0% in the past 20 years. Fortunately, we have scientists constantly working on artificial intelligence, and the tenth generation of robot, which will be introduced today, is born!"

"Right! This generation of robot is totally personalized. You don't need to worry that you don't have your partner fund or your children accompanying you. You can buy a wife or husband, chap or lass, choose whichever you like!"

Mrs. White called the black man. She didn't want a new husband. She wanted her "family" to reunion.

VII

Mr. White (fixed), Verna (fixed) and Mrs. White (healthy) were sitting on the beach. Verna was drinking a cup of orange juice, with her dark, wet curl stamped on each cheek.

"It's so good that we three can sit together again," said Mrs. White, "I love reunion."

"What do you mean by reunion?" asked Mr. White, "have we been apart?"

Mrs. White paused a little bit, thinking of this new family she bought 5 years ago. The invention of artificial intelligence was really a magical thing: she no longer had to argue with her boyfriend, for her "husband" now was designed to please her. Nor did she have to worry about the "children thing", since she could buy how many children she wanted. The company between human was always fragile: even children could break up with their parents, let alone couples. So she'd rather buy a robot family to accompany her, although the company was sometimes mortal. Once she heard the "ten, nine, eight⋯" sound, she knew that this journey of company was about to come to an end.

But is it a company limited in a period?

No. As long as the mistakes can be fixed, she can stay with her Mr. White and Verna, and enjoy the immortal accompany that only exists between human and robots.

"No, darling," she smiled, and answered in a delightful voice, "we have never been apart—"

—And we will never be.

（作者学校：北京大学附属中学）

本文为2017年"北大培文杯"决赛参赛文

> **作者的话**

"被重力束缚的人类。"

必须承认，本篇灵感来源于《机动战士敢达 UC》，这个故事就是在原作背景下结合我自身的想象创作而成的。

即使人类在某个未来能将肉身送入太空，地球的重力仍束缚着大部分人的心灵。

"敢达 UC"系列不仅是科幻，还描绘了一幅在"宇宙世纪"（Universal Century, UC）的语境下太空后殖民主义与平民主义反击的图景。我们又将如何面对新纪元的不平等、观念冲突与更可怕的太空战争呢？诞生于宇宙中的"新人类"（New-Type）们，究竟能否与旧世代人类达成和解呢？

在结尾处，"我"仍不能领悟这其中的意义；在两个纪元的交接之时，"我"能做的唯有闭上眼睛去想象未来。

现在，我把答案留给你们。尽管前路迷茫，但不要忘记，宇宙世纪（UC）也是独角兽（Unicorn）的世纪、可能性之兽的世纪。

FIVE SECONDS TO THE UNIVERSAL CENTURY

赵炜

"Good afternoon, my fellow citizens on Earth and those in the New Colonies. Now it is 23:30 in Greenwich Mean Time, and I feel privileged to be here, on behalf of the Earth Federation, to send our best wishes for the coming Universal Century…" Prime Minister Marcenas was addressing his featured speech on air, attractive but ostentatious, arousing a strong disgust from my heart though I was not on the spot. In fact, I was watching the live broadcast on the Colony Moon Ⅲ, a remote body from the Earth. It was for several years that I had been abandoned and forced to work here for my family.

Having suffered a prolonged baptism of fire, former states on Earth came into agreement that divergence was eliminated and that all should unite as a sole Federation. Such a proposition had proved beneficial to humankind's future. Furthermore, the Federation decided to explore the space for more dwellings and resources. Since then, mass immigration projects had been successfully under process towards the *terra incognita*. Certainly, the ultimate goal of those manoeuvres, I knew, was nothing but to abandon the poor or the inferior and set up a paradise for the sake of the elite. I knew it well, what this could mean to us, the people forced to work to support a family.

I looked at the watch. It's 23:40 then, still twenty minutes before the New Era, that was a conversion from AD to UC calendar. "Huh-huh, may the deceitful ceremony be ruined by those Zeon soldiers." My fellow worker said, then laughed. In fact, most of the poor guys laboring on Colony Moons recently learned about the Zeon Army: they had planted a bomb in the space station serving as the Hall. When the clock struck 0:00, the symbol of the very beginning of UC calendar, the bomb would blow up the Hall and troops from Zeon would march on towards the Earth from the three Colony Moons under Zeon Republic's control. It was predictable that Zeon rebellion against the Federation was approaching.

Although there were many who long to overthrow the Federal reign, such an uncertainty of future that war would lead to worried me a lot. Currently, laws and regulations for the New Colonies were in discussion by the Federation. As the Constitution wrote, the eight Colony Moons were subjected to the Federation and thus the Colonial Parliament should be sponsored by Federal officials. However, various restrictions and heavy taxation on the New Colony had resulted in desperate abandoned people joining a military group against such an inequality and tyranny. Then the Zeon Republic was born, in name of Zionism, the pursuit for home after the diaspora of the ancient Jews. Encouraged by Zeon, all the Moons had in reality turned into quasi-autonomous regions. Also, recently a hearsay was prevailing that some of the human beings in space would be strengthened both physically and mentally by the new environment, and that those so-called New-Types may easily master high-tech weapons and finally end the rulings. "Maybe great change will have taken place in the new Universal

Century." I thought.

"Oh, and now it has come to 23:55, we have the last five minutes for our A.D. … I want to tell you what the new Era means to me. In fact, U.C. is supposed to stand for the Universe Century, yet we think 'Universal' not only means an epoch for human to explore the space, but also one century when all citizens share equality." "What nonsense! What ON EARTH do you know about the universality? All of you are no more than bloody tyrants depriving the legal rights of Colony people! You wicked!" A demonstrator at the Hall shouted at the Minister, and was arrested immediately.

Yes, what he had spoken out was right the truth. A sense of bitterness caught me.

The Minister continued to address, "finally there are ten seconds left for the New Era, why not countdown together!"

"Ten…" Ten represented the ten Articles of the Constitution, which could ironically be compared to the Ten Commandments for Zionists and now the Zeon people. All promises were fake to us, I knew.

"Nine…" Nine meant that, with a long-term nuclear war among former nations, there existed only nine percent of resources left for human to use. And thus the Federation decided to drive out lower-class people from the Earth in approval of its own benefits.

"Eight…" Eight was the number of existing Colony Moons, and every Moon populated almost ten percent of human population. Fortunately, the eight Moons were determined to unite and fight for their rights in this vast universe.

"Seven…" After seven years of the catastrophic war, people on

Earth agreed to have peace, for which they set up the Earth Federation, but no one would foresee the chaotic world nowadays.

"Six…" It was said that the Zeon Republic built six gigantic military robots called Mobile Suit. They were considered as the symbol of the Zeon Rebellion and victory for the New-Types and abandoned people who suffered from the space diaspora.

With the countdown for ten to six, I reminded smoothly of such things in mind. Yet as for the last five seconds, I would like to close my eyes.

No wonder the bomb was to function, no wonder the Zeon troops would march on, and no wonder the beginning of the Universal Century was to mark the prelude of Zeon rebellion for equal rights between Earth and New Colonies…

Still afraid of the coming war, I had no other choice, and all of us had not realized all the meanings.

"Goodbye, Anno Domini."

But what if it would end up with being too far gone and endless regrets for what we had done?

"Yea, even though I walk through the valley of the shadow of death, I will fear no evil: for thou art with me; thy rod and thy staff they comfort me." feeling the tranquility of the space I held my existence in, I recalled myself of such a solemn psalm.

Five seconds to the Universal Century.

I closed my eyes, though I hadn't realized all the meanings.

（作者学校：广东省广州市执信中学）
本文为2017年"北大培文杯"决赛参赛文

> **作者的话**
>
> 从 *The Idea of "Fo Xi" Youth* 到 *Label*，是我与小培结缘的见证，也是书写自我、创意写作带给我的收获。以角色之口诉说心中所想，通过故事展示对世界的理解，是我钟情小说这一创作形式的理由。我的决赛作文尽力去探讨在人工智能高速发展的今天，面对越来越多的伦理问题与道德问题、矛盾与挑战，平凡的个体会做出怎样的抉择？在结尾，我给出了自己的答案；在未来，还有更多未结的疑问等待着我去找寻发现。参加培文，让我的写作更加自由，愿创意之梦永远青春！

DEAR MR. ROBOT-I

徐仪筱

Dear Eddie Harrison,

I feel awfully sorry to inform you that the Robot-II will be recalled by our company in two days. Though I hate this, my friend, hearing your sister's tearful complaining every day is indeed unbearable.

You can choose to pay all the services before May 17th, or you can apply for a loan in our company. If I were you, Eddie, getting ready to pay a large fortune as quickly as possible is the best choice, or you

Dear Mr. Robot-I

will have to pay the money for the injury of the robot's function.

You know, Robot-II is our latest robot for companying, especially for the old and those who are afflicted with the loss of their beloved one. When you decided to buy the Robot, by virtue of your sister's vulnerable mental condition, we advised you to choose more character labels in the robot to deal with different situations.

You paid for the highest.

It has characters including "Outgoing" "Excellent quality for sports" "Energetic" "Sensitive", ¥5000 000 in total. That's the most apparent and visible capacity from her died son, David. During our experiments, we all believed that our dear Robot-II would surely heal her sadness for David and helped her to begin a new life.

Am I too proud of our technique? I remember that night, after our final security check, I promised you everything will be all right. We never doubted it, for Robot-II with the four characters you chose behaved just like David. They have the same interest, and David would even go back to school and won the football match, just as David did before!

A month later we sent our staff to your sister's house, at that time everything seems fine. Madam Harrison and her new "son" just finished their loitering in the street. We talked a few minutes and the staff began to check the system. To our satisfaction, we didn't find any record about your sister related to complaint or argument. "He is a talkative boy," said your sister, "He can talk about the football game and some teenage things all day long with me. It's so sweet! David always did this."

As Mrs. Harrison gave us a satisfying feedback, we reached an agreement that we would come back to recheck the robot three months later, instead of one month. Our staff seemed a little unease, but I was so busy answering my phone that I didn't notice it.

Three months later, I received the report of our poor Robot-II. "Its system is completely a mess and I can't imagine what she has done to him," said the engineer in charge of this, "tell her machine-head brother to pay another 2 000 dollars, or we will bring it back in minutes!"

"I have expected this." I remembered you looked quite embarrassed. "But we shouldn't blame her… poor Hannah, she has lost everything." It suddenly stroke me that maybe the data and information carried by Robot-II need updating, since our robot was "Energetic", your sister must be tired of hearing football game that had finished long before or news about a washed-up star. So I updated it, this update cost you 1 000 dollars.

I know you're worried about your sister, but as the manager of the company, I have to say that a few minutes a month by her side was indeed a curse. The last time I saw her, she sat still in her chair like a sculpture. I hardly called the emergency. She was holding a diary, shabby and broken, but her eyes shone with proud. That afternoon, we talked a lot. She said this was written by David when he was three years old. "He loves many things, too many that even for me to remember. But he is more than those matters," whispered your sister, "He wrote his experiences in the book about how he got to form a hobby and gain knowledge. Meeting new people… he had his dreams, he had his future, but the robot has nothing. It had no past, no future, only a present controlled by some silly labels."

Dear Mr. Robot-I

I found Robot-II outside house a few meters away. At that time I suddenly remembered that it had a label of "Sensitive".

I called our staff. He said— after the examination— Robot-II couldn't stay with your sister anymore. Records show that Mrs. Harrison cried every day and sometimes she even threw bad words at poor Robot-II. The staff showed his sorry to me that five months before, when your sister asked him with excitement how Robot-II behaved like her son, our honest friend said it was all about the four character labels you chose.

"And she stood dead with shock, then she began to tremble like flickering leaves⋯ I'm sorry. I'm sorry⋯ I have never expected this⋯ I shouldn't have told her⋯"The staff said.

Therefore, the Robot-II will finish all the services soon, I have told you everything about your sister and Robot-II, not leaving a single detail. I hope to tell you that you have tried your best. This is not your fault. You paid the highest and we sent our best robot and engineer. Sometimes, we can't pretend to believe a replacement can solve all the problems. Hopefully, your sister will find her way to get out of the shadow. I will take care of her. Best wishes.

Yours sincerely,
Daniel

I finished writing the letter. It was noon, thankfully everybody was sleeping so that nobody would notice me. Unfortunately, the minute I walked out of the door, a huge voice caught me.

"Hey Daniel! Where are you going?"

No, here came my partner. No news could escape her, I had to give in.

"Umm, just sending a letter to my friend?"

"Oh, come on, who will send letter at this time? You must have something unwilling to let anyone else know, aren't you? God, I thought we were friends…"

"Please, that's enough!" I sighed, "I'm telling the truth!"

"Then whom are you writing to?"

I hesitated for a moment.

"Eddie Harrison."

"What, another Harrison? Well, the only Harrison we know is Hannah Harrison. Poor lady, her parents died, leaving her a robot as a companion, but the robot's system went wrong only after one year. Is that her?"

"Yes, you are right. But now it's worse than you can see. That's why I'm secretly writing this letter."

"Wait, she has no relatives and her financial condition is not that good, who paid the money for her? Who is that 'Eddie'?"

"Eddie?" I said slowly, "Eddie is the name of her first robot."

Silence, only silence, I had to go on.

"Her first robot's system went wrong, remember? Eddie, or Robot-I, whichever you like, suddenly had human feelings. He thought he was Hannah's brother which caused tons of problems. We had no choice but to bring him back. He was now staying in some top scientists' laboratory, being examined every day. They have even torn him apart once, but he still remembered Hannah, when he woke up, the first thing for him was to ask where his sister is."

My partner was in tears.

"But recently, he came to accept the fact that he was not human, but just a robot. One day he even asked me how much he valued, which made me feel a sense of relief. However, in a few days he told me he wanted to sell himself and buy a new robot for his heartbroken sister, as he knew Hannah's son died accidentally. He was excited to know that he was worth quite a lot so he could finally do something for his sister."

"Clearly," I added, "It's undoubtedly forbidden. You can see how stupid I am. I cheated him and promised that his will would come true. In fact, I paid all the money myself. But he didn't know, $5 003 000, a large fortune. You think I am the most stupid person in the world, don't you? Now I am even going to write this letter to him, urging him to pay for it, pretending nothing has happened…"

"Does Eddie… sorry, the Robot, has its label?" My partner asked.

"Only one label, that's love."

I walked away, but at exactly that time I heard a voice from the other side of the aisle, which frozed me to the ground.

"Robot-Ⅲ, with the label of 'compassionate', works in good condition."

（作者学校：山东省泰安第二中学）
本文为2018年"北大培文杯"决赛参赛文

> **作者的话**
>
> 我爱好英语，也喜欢数理化。学习之余，我喜欢打篮球、乒乓球，下象棋、围棋，听唱英文歌曲，也喜欢跟父母一起散步，交流所思所想。这次创意作文大赛，我收获颇多，感悟颇多，它唤醒了我沉睡许久的创意种子——创意是改变我们生活现状的力量之源！我会更加笃定地前行：宝剑锋从磨砺出，梅花香自苦寒来！感谢"北大培文杯"这一舞台，让我们尽情地书写创意；感谢大赛工作人员的辛勤付出，让我们稍纵即逝的创意得以留存；感谢我的英语老师——金胜霞老师的指导；感谢父母的支持。

INDESTRUCTIBLE HEART

肖易佳

The Catastrophe

"My boy, it's time to go to bed." It was the voice of my father.

"Okay, okay." I replied, closing the door behind me.

Lying on my bed, I just couldn't fall asleep.

I felt something bad was going on, but I just couldn't tell what it was exactly…

"Dong— Dong—!" The thunder outside was loud enough to wake up the dead.

"Damn weather!" I exclaimed, getting out of my bed. No sooner had I reached the windows than thousands of lightning flashed across the dark sky, making the world as light as daytime.

"I am not the only victim, nobody can fall asleep…"

"Ah—" A scream came from the outside. "That must be the poor beggar, Brain." I thought to myself, looking out of the window.

"Ah—" Another scream came out of my mouth. A bird-like spaceship was descending, slowly and steadily.

Everyone was as frightened as me. Suddenly, the spaceship turned into a giant.

"Sorry, I don't want to wake you up, but the earth is my colony now!" The voice was as ugly as the giant himself. "There is no escape!" He shouted. The ground began to shake, millions of walls surrounded us…

The Panic

The sun was rising in the east, making us warm, but our hearts were as cold as ice. "Are we going to die?" I forced a smile, so bitterly.

"All the cities and villages have been surrounded by thousands of walls, which are made from energy, so it's no use striking the walls. The harder you strike, the higher they will become…" Upset, I turned off the TV and went out.

On the square, a large crowd of people had already gathered

around the monument.

"We are dying!" A woman cried. "No escape…" another woman added.

"No, I don't want to die—" I fell to the ground and lost my senses…

The Help

"My boy, wake up!"

I opened my eyes, only to find an old man approaching me with something golden in his hand.

"It's the Devil, he will take advantage of your weakness, like dishonesty, selfishness. The only way to survive is to unite and trust each other. You humans have the greatest weapon, that is the indestructible heart!" He said, handing the golden heart to me.

"Are you God?!"

The old man nodded his head. Then, everything was gone…

The Union

I came back to life, Ah… Is it a dream? Hmm? Something hard in my hand?

The golden heart, the word "Indestructible" was carved in it!

……

The president got the news.

The union was organized.

The people united.

The golden heart shone.

……

We were human. We had indestructible hearts!

The Plan

"The golden heart is the key…" I explained.

Soldiers were ordered to strike the wall with the golden heart.

The walls shook terribly, people burst into cheers!

But wait!

The wall grew higher and thicker!

……

The Trust

"My dear president, we are a union, but we are NOT a team. We don't trust each other. How can a heart full of doubt be indestructible?! The Devil is just taking advantage of our weakness."

I gave a speech to the world.

People were changing, and miracles happened.

Nobody doubted.

Nobody lied.

Nobody fought.

Nobody stole.

……

We were changing, and we could actually feel something good was going on…

The golden heart grew bigger and brighter day by day! Our hearts grew stronger and purer.

We would be the final winner!

The Challenge

We were running out of food.

There were people dying every day, but nobody had even the slightest thought of stealing or robbing. We were a team! A TEAM!

The God nodded his head.

The Devil was on his way to our Earth.

The Battle

"You must have made all efforts to break the walls. As I can see, the walls are much higher and thicker. For my first meal, whose soul will have the honor to be eaten first?" The Devil said scornfully.

His wicked gaze fell on me…

"Are you honored?"

"Yes!" I replied immediately, without a second thought.

"I will take your soul out of your body softly."

"I am honored, NOT because of you Devil, but BECAUSE I could die for people and die a heroic death!"

The golden heart shone like the sun.

I could feel my soul being pulled out.

"Goodbye, my parents. Goodbye, my friends."

"A soul without weakness?" The Devil shouted in surprise, "Then how can I eat it, how can I bite it…"

The Devil tried several other people, but stopped in vain.

"Damn!" He turned around and wanted to flee.

Too late!

The golden heart was even brighter than the sun, and it opened. Holy and pure light rays shrouded the Devil. "Let me free!" The Devil was absorbed into the heart and couldn't escape.

And the walls? They were as crispy as chips when we touched them. All the walls had been broken down…

And the golden heart? It was sent into the National Museum and would be perfectly preserved there. It will remind future generations of the indestructible heart and the broken walls.

The Lesson

The indestructible heart has come.

The Devil has gone.

The world is now a paradise full of virtues.

The world is now a paradise full of happiness.

I also learned something different…

Every human being, no matter who he is, inside him, there is a world. The Devil is greedy, dishonest, false and doubtful. If we don't take this seriously, he will build walls to eat our soul, we will lose our family, friends, happiness and success.

But human being have the greatest weapon, as God said, an indestructible heart. The heart should be filled with trust, honesty and love. ALL kinds of VIRTUES. Then, the walls will be broken down by our hearts, with ease.

So, if everybody can purify his soul, our hearts will be indestructible, and the walls will be broken down. And this world will be perfect without any Devil…

The heart shines!

The God smiles!

The Devil flees!

The happiness comes!

The walls broken down!

The world becomes a paradise!

The sun is still rising in the east, making us warm, and this time our hearts are happy and warm. As you can see, our hearts are indestructible!

How wonderful!

（作者学校：新疆维吾尔自治区乌鲁木齐市第一中学）

本文为2016年"北大培文杯"决赛参赛文

Dear Mr. Robot-I

> **作者的话**
>
> 受家人影响，我自幼对历史感兴趣，因此读了不少中外史书和人物传记；又是一个纯天然理科生，科幻作品自然颇对自己胃口。既为严谨而又具有史诗感的作品着迷，又折服于天马行空、有据可考的想象。一直是托尔金《指环王》和刘慈欣《三体》的狂热粉丝，因而见缝插针地尝试着在自己的一篇作品中如同他们一样，不仅仅是在讲一个故事，更是在构建一个全新的世界——我的世界。

HOPE

董觉非

Fifty feet… forty feet… I walked towards our base, painfully and exhausted.

Thirty feet… twenty feet… I knew I was bleeding out.

There's only ten feet left to go, but it seemed to be the longest length I've ever seen.

Ten, nine, eight, seven, six… I fell down, and struggled to crawl forward, feet by feet. A strange feeling stuck me that I couldn't make it to go home.

To be frank, it was not my life that mattered, but the seedling in my container which was, to some degree, the hope and future for human beings.

About five hours ago, when the elevator stopped at the basement, I walked out and was immediately surrounded by officers who were busy checking my equipment.

I could hardly conceal my excitement and curiosity due to the fact that I would be one of the first men to go back to the ground after the disastrous war.

No sooner had their work was done, than the door above opened.

I climbed onto the ground, and for the first time in my life, I saw what the world was like five hundred years after the World War Ⅲ.

The nuclear war, which had brought destruction to human civilization, not only created deadly radiation, but also formed dusts that blotted out the sky and the sun, making the surface of our planet a place where no living creatures could survive.

As a consequence, those lucky survivors had no choice but to live and rebuild our world under the ground, but of course, on a much smaller scale.

But with the explosive growth of population, the shortage of all kinds of resources arose, causing the spread of worries and dismay.

That was why I, who knew nothing about the world above us before the mission was sent to the ground.

Armed with heavy equipment which was designed to protect me from radiation, I looked around, and all I could see through my breath mask was oppressive black.

Black clouds, black soil, black ruins… The war had destroyed our

Dear Mr. Robot-I

home completely.

Despite I was told again and again that there would be nothing left on the ground, I was a little disappointed for deep in my heart, I thought I would have the chance to see the so-called plants.

Yes, plants, real plants. Not those fake ones in our basement whose only job was to absorb nutrition from nutrient and kept us away from starvation. The real plants must be juicy and full of vigor, just like what was written in our history book.

But apparently, no plants could survive in such a terrible environment.

I kept walking through the empty street. The buildings beside me were more than two meters tall. They once stood for the symbol of the prosperity and power of human. But now, they were more likely to be the tombstones that human made for themselves.

"The dust cloud has become much thinner, so sunlight can reach the ground, the radiation has also weakened a lot… but… visibility is still poor, and the radiation is deadly high… There's no sign of life… I don't think it's the right time to get back… Request for the permission of getting back to base." I was reporting when I heard the sound of water.

I followed the sound and reached the bank of a river. Badly polluted by the nuclear weapons, the water had become disgusting. But to my surprise and delight, I spotted something I was looking forward to seeing for years.

I approached it slowly and slightly, fearing any other movement would make it fade away. I sat beside it, observing carefully.

I could hardly believe my eyes, but they were telling me the truth.

It was a plant, a real plant with green leaves and clustered flower buds. It seemed to be the only other kind of color in the black world. I remembered our teacher once told us that plants were the greatest living beings in the world. Under no circumstance they would spare no effects to grow bravely, no matter how poor the soil was or how little sunlight they could get. They never gave in or gave up. They just grew until one day they were able to spread their seeds. I used to doubt it, but now I might have changed my mind.

It suddenly struck me that it was my responsibility to take it back to our base. I had to show it to my people to prove that miracle existed and tell them: if a small plant could make it survive, why can't we?

I believed it would change something.

To drive worries and anxieties away.

To bring hope and vitality back.

To cure the wounds and wipe the tears.

If god did exist, the plant must be his gift for all his people.

I took out a container, and placed the plant into it with great care, just like a devout believer holding a holy cup.

I was about to leave when I found with scare that an odd creature with three faces was standing in my way.

The radiation not only killed a tremendous number of creatures, but also affected many animals' genes as well, turning them into dangerous and aggressive monsters.

And unfortunately it seemed to be interested in the plant as well. Staring at its sharp teeth and paws, my legs began to tremble.

I was so far away from our base that I could not expect any

Dear Mr. Robot-I

assistance. Maybe I would survive if I dropped the container and ran away as fast as I could, but⋯ if I did so, the people living underground might never have the chance to see it— the hope bringer.

Images occurred to me that a boy sat in a small classroom, looking at a picture of a lily which stood for hope before the war. I could read the eagerness in his eyes. I could also recognize the boy was me.

Then the boy faded, groups of people appeared. Some were sobbing, some were quarreling, and some were fighting for just a can of food.

Finally I saw some plants planting in a greenhouse. All of them were green, juicy, and full of vigor. Many people gathered to see it. Life was still tough in the underground world, but hope existed in their eyes.

I knew what I had to do. To run away I may live at least for a while ,but one day when I was dying in my bed, I would willing to give all my days for a chance to come back here and fight for our hope and dream.

The war⋯ The radiation⋯ The shortage of supplies⋯ They might take our lives, but they would never take our hope.

I pulled out my knife. "Come on, you beast." I said to myself.

Those were all I remembered when I struggled to stand up, walking slowly to our base, holding the container firmly.

Ten, nine, eight, seven, six⋯

There only five feet left. But I knew I could not make it.

But sooner or later another pioneer like me would be sent to the ground. They would mourn for me and found the plant. I could not imagine how excited they would be when they saw the container. They would bring it home, taking good care of it. They would bring hope home.

My eyesight began to blur when the gate opened.

I was home.

So did the hope.

（作者学校：重庆市第十八中学）

本文为 2017 年"北大培文杯"决赛参赛文

> **作者的话**
>
> 姚东妮，文科妹子一枚，爱生活，爱旅行，爱阅读，爱写作，喜欢尝试新鲜事物，敢于追求自己的梦想。
>
> 初试英语短篇小说写作，聆听着指尖在键盘上敲击的声音，享受着灵魂在天马行空的想象中遨游。每每自己所写的场景浮现在大脑中，犹如上演一部惊世骇俗的世纪大片。在才思枯竭时，也曾尝试阅读经典书籍、看看英文电影，找寻灵感。
>
> 因为热爱，所以坚持……

THE RIGHT AND THE LEFT

姚东妮

As everyone knows, the wall of Berlin was broken down and made people from both the East Germany and the West Germany reunited. But this is from your world, not mine.

Who am I? Maybe you can regard me as a human who live in the parallel time with you.

You maybe wonder how I could know your world and history. It's a long story that needs to be dated on a "normal" day.

Do you live in the same world?

"Welcome back! Have a taste on the new ice cream I just made." "No, thanks." I said coldly. The woman in front of me was my step-mother, who always seemed to be good with me. But, I hated her, not only because she wanted to replace my mom, but also because she came from the Right. She is a Right.

I shut my door, turned on the computer and surfed on the internet. Feeling bored, I typed some letters randomly and went into a girl's "blog" which I never knew.

"January 16, 2032— my father set out to the outer space for all of us. Everyone in the world expects for his good news. I'm sure he will."

Set out to the outer space? Everyone in the world? Why don't I know about it?

"What is it talking about?" I typed quickly under her passage.

"How couldn't you know? The president announced it on the TV this morning that we are going to move to another star."

"Wait, the President? At which side?"

"Side?"

"I mean Right or Left?"

"Right or Left?"

We had said many things but it seemed we didn't live in the same world. I didn't know what she talked about and all that I had said was unfamiliar to her.

Dear Mr. Robot-I

The Right and the Left

"Well. I just guess, perhaps you live in the parallel time. Dad set forward once in a time. But they are unsure whether it really exists."

That's interesting. Parallel time? Whatever, the world she lived in seemed more amazing.

We talked a lot about the world she lives in and the world of mine. I told her about my family and of course, the Right and the Left.

"In my world, people were born with a date and were given the option on which side they belong to. Right people like being together. People laugh a lot and sometimes weep . While on the Left, people like to be alone, calm, and they hardly express their feelings."

Due to this, it built a wall between the Right and the Left long time ago. Many people from the Left tried to run to the Right and Rights climbed over to the Left. "So, the wall was broken down for few years which made the world in chaos. "I said and sighed.

"Wow! that's interesting. It is similar to the East and West Germany!" She said and then told me about the history about her world.

"I'll go to the interests of Berlin Wall tomorrow." She added.

"Maybe you can try to get along with the Right people. Begin it from your step-mother. Maybe, if all of you can be reunited like Germans, you will see the advantages of it."

"Maybe, see you tomorrow."

The Wall

The girl went to the Berlin wall and I also went to the "wall" the next day. Children were running near the "wall" and couples were chatting happily. After it broke down, a park was built as a reminder of that day. I just went there once with my mom. I saw the little boy (me) holding his mother's hand and she said to me. "There were no Right and Left long time ago. People lived together happily. But some people hated others personally. So they built the "wall" to distinguish Right and Left. Forced by the army, they separated families to Right and Left."

"But, you should know, my dear son. All of us belong to a big family long long ago. We should be reunited one day." Mom suddenly disappeared.

Sun hanging in the sky and it was so bright and warm.

Someone held up my hands, just like mom held me long ago. I turned back— it was my step-mother. She smiled at me as before. But this time I didn't hate her as before.

I approached the "wall" which never existed. "Thank you." I whispered, but I knew the girl in your world can hear me and I seemed to see the girl behind the "wall" smiling at me.

Right, the "wall" never existed in the world, neither in the past nor in the future, neither in my world nor in your world.

（作者学校：河北省石家庄市第二中学）
本文为 2016 年 "北大培文杯" 决赛参赛文

Dear Mr. Robot-I

> **作者的话**
>
> 写作于我，是个相当矛盾的事物。写不出来的时候，字斟句酌，有如挤牙膏一般；灵感闪过的时候，又是一番酣畅淋漓的享受。曾经以为的这种叫作灵感的东西，或许，是因为在意，是因为心里有声音在呐喊，于是结成文字流淌出来。写这篇文章的那个暑假，我第一次比较深入地接触古代文化，看到西塞罗的"吾每读柏拉图，无不泣涕于苏格拉底之死"，隐约有些悲凉。几千年了，人类对彼此的敌意却没有消减，一次次重蹈覆辙；所幸人类还有爱、有善、有共情、有过往的残片，留下的故事和思考遂化为文字，成了文学。当人们迷失前路时，这些淌过时间的文字或许会引起共鸣，或许会唤起心中的爱和善，鼓舞人类朝着更好的未来走去吧。

BACK TO ZERO

谭力珲

"Ten, nine, eight, seven, six… Did I tell you, young man, that I had worked this way all these past years?" The old statistician murmured, pushing out one of his few weak breaths left, and then led a severe series of coughs.

"Yes, that's where we stopped last time…" Frank held out his hand, trying to make the old man feel a bit better. He liked him. Not many scholars felt like doing research these days, after all, there was no Ivory Tower anymore. "To ameliorate," he thought, "a word of considerable antiquity."

"That was when I was born," the old statistician paused for a moment, as if struggling to pick up more of his scattered memory of the old days, "on my day to come, there were around ten great wars over the world: each could cause megadeaths, just like the Second World War in the ancient time. Everyone was poor enough then: one meal a day, porridge, synthetic sausages, and pork fortnightly. My mother was a wise woman. She could read Latin, so she gave me my name, Decem, hoping that someday I could count the wars back to zero. You know, from ten." He then stopped, trying to recall more.

Frank remembered last time he came to visit Decem. It was before the battle, the Last Battle, they called it. But as far as he could recall, it was the ninth time they used the name. "The ninth Last Battle." He whispered to himself.

It was June, 3017 AD, more than seven millennia after the first civilization ever appeared on this fragile planet. The pioneers to build up society for the first time, those men and women long buried in the sands, were they afraid of killing and death? Would they be frightened, that millions of lives could become dead bodies within breath time, and that civilizations could be wiped off in a blink of eye? Frank thought, then let out a sigh. The wars continued, though it had been almost five score years after Decem was named unusual.

"As I was about to enter the university," Decem started again. His weak but firm voice dragged Frank out of his own thoughts, "the School, as they call it now, they don't even know the word university! I chose to major in mathematics and statistics. Numbers, emm, I thought they could tell me the answer, and demonstrate to the world what they should value……"

"Did you get the answer then?" Frank asked. He just received the report that the Last Battle would begin and that he was left with little time.

"Oh, young man. The numbers did tell me how devastating wars could be and had been. But they just didn't believe in that anymore... You know, people in the past believed in money, so they started wars to rob it, but now they don't even believe in that! Numbers lost their power. What do they want now? They start to enjoy this. Those who have armies long to conquer; those with guns itch to kill……" he let out another series of coughs. As he calmed down, he started again, "'That couldn't be the key.' I thought at that time. That's almost seventy years ago. Then I went to consult sociology, economics and… emm, psychology. To my disappointment, the number of wars those days even doubled. They didn't count them down, they counted up."

"Ten years later, I met Lily. She was just like her name, so pure and so clean, even in such a world. She was a little melancholy sometimes, though."

Frank grew a bit anxious. The mobile reporter had rung a few times. It was time to leave.

"Find Dr. Decem," Brad told him so before he let out his last breath, "he could tell you the key… that we've been looking for…"

He must find this key.

"Don't be anxious, young man. Quickly ripe, quickly rotten. The ancient Romans had known this." Decem continued, "The point's coming. Once, Lily told me, 'how could they shoot a life that resembles themselves that much without even feeling any pain? They must have sold their heart to the demon. They don't love. They lost their most precious gift.' You know what, I got the point I'd been searching for years! That's love, that is conscience."

Frank seemed disappointed. He came here for an answer, for a key, not just two words. He stood up, tears in his eyes. "I failed to find the key to peace. Brad, will you forgive me?" He thought, looking up into the sky, grey and cloudy.

"That is you." Decem gripped his sleeve, and continued, "That is your friends."

"I started a plan then, and later a university project. With Lily, we adopted 50 boys and girls who lost their families in the war. The professors like us cared for them, played with them and taught them the wisdom of human beings and the nature of the world. We brought you up and groups of families. We taught you to love, to forgive, to create…" Decem's breath weakened, but he continued his words, "I then hid behind, doing my research in warfare, trying to count them down. Ten, nine, eight, seven, six… and now it's one… I hope you could bring it back to zero. Bye…" His voice fell, and then there was a silence, only the wind murmured.

Frank stood there, frozen. He got the answer. He did not.

A mellifluous melody drifted in through the half-opened window. He followed it and rushed downstairs. The soldiers and villagers were singing. That was the old song, he could recognize it, the ancient chant— *Fine Tomorrow.*

"Now it comes," he thought, "back to zero."

（作者学校：重庆市育才中学）

本文为2017年"北大培文杯"决赛参赛文

作者的话

在下武阅海。阅海，意为读万卷书、行万里路、阅人无数。读万卷书，功在光阴；行万里路，暂凭家庭；阅人无数，校塾常新呵。会古都盛集，可以读书行路阅人，与有荣焉！

却怨白驹过隙，已然欢欣悲歌。幸得以文属友，惟恋清风微抚，昆明湖畔。与那云烟，酹双月。

念那年博雅塔下挥斥方遒，现可安好？只愿天下学子大展宏图！顺颂时祺。

TEN YOUNG HEARTS OF RISING SUN

武阅海

A pleasant summer dawn came again! Birds twittered their favorite songs while braches and leaves were cutting the sunshine into random pieces of light spot on the ground, which they wanted to use as greetings of a day.

As for me, I was just like those happy creatures inside the trees. Putting my headphones on, I started to enjoy my favorite *Jasmine Flowers*. Suddenly I sensed a faint sound of a vehicle movement to which I didn't pay enough attention. Then I was hit and was knocked down to the ground. I saw blood everywhere, horrible scars of my own added to my fear.

I was waiting to die and closed my eyes. I wanted to make full use of the rest of my life to look back my passed years of happiness and frustration when a scene that I should never forget happened.

"Young man, you are to enjoy your best time sooner." There was a voice spreading from the sky above my head.

"I···" I thought that I must be insane but replied.

"Old people are oppressed by the fear of death, in the youngster there is a justification for this feeling. Young men who have reason to fear that they will be killed as teens may justifiably feel bitter in the thought that they have been cheated of the best things that life has to offer. However, it's unfair for you guy to die so soon. I decide to offer ten scenarios to you. You will be content."

"Who··· who are you?"

"The spirit of nature."

I

Suddenly, I felt like that I had no weight at all. Looking around, I realized that I was in a space capsule in which men are of zero-gravity if the shuttle is traveling around the orbit of a planet. I swam around by specially made magnetic boots. I got near to the operating bridge and saw the words of "Sky Palace • No.1• China". "Wow!!!Wow!!!" I couldn't help myself and shouted out! "This is the tenth shuttle of my motherland!!"

"Maybe I can realize my dream here." I thought. "Take me to Sigma Tauri." I said. "Roger." Distortion field generated. Thermomechanical yielded stabilizer online. Sub space worm hole expanded. Preliminary ignition motioned. Gravity analyses updated to Database Lip links. 17 minutes to destination. Nice trip! That's true! Technologies from fictions now ARE MASTERED by us!

17 minutes later, I was at Sigma Tauri with tears floating down my face.

II

I was sitting in a desert in the second scenario.

Nine cavalries appeared in front of me. One of them got down from his horse and said: "Traveler! You know where to find a lake, a cactus and an eagle which is eating a snake?"

"Aztec!" I was shocked and thought. "Are you Mexicans who are seeking a place to settle down and taking tiring migration following god's command?"

"Yes! Dude! We indeed found one in Tenochtitlan. But it was destroyed by the Spanish Conquers! They forced us to find another city, no, all the cities are in ruins."

"Believe in your sagas!" I encouraged them. "Mexico will be prosperous again!"

III

"It's Tian an." I had no time to think because someone pushed me to hide behind bushes.

"You are crazy! Foreigners are looting around! You want to die?!!"

I watched down following the finger's direction of the man who saved me. Banners were waving around, among which I saw flags of Briton, France, Germany, Österreich, America, Italy, Russia and Japan. "Oh, no! It's the beginning of 20th Century now. People of China are suffering."

I looked around and saw a flintlock musket. I picked it up and went back to speak to the man, "let's protect our citizens!" The man looked at me, hesitated. "I admit that I'm a soldier, but main troops have withdrawn. We can't⋯" "Then give me your rifle." I said coldly, glaring at his eyes.

"It's better than this rusty musket." He dropped his equipment and ran away.

"Let's make a stand." I murmured, putting on my bayonet.

"Bullets, fierce their breast plates and penetrate their souls!" I jumped out to fire."You can defeat our army, but never our honor!"

A cuirassier charged at my flank and I blacked out.

IV

Even in scenario 4, I could sense the pain in my waist.

"Ok, tenth optimization of 'Tian Gong' series. Nine Mexico cavalries, the army of eight nations, what will be the seventh?" I thought.

"Stranger, where are you from? Why are you in my palace? " A crowned man said. "Who are you?" "How dare you! I'm a Fredrick. The emperor of The Holly Roman Empire and the owner of entire Habsburg!"

"Yes? you stole the name of Senatus Populusque Romanesque. Julian Caesar won't forgive you easily! He will penalize you with his legionaries!"

"Catch him!" Fredrick lost his temper. "You are challenging imperial authority!" I had to run at that moment, but I was confused: where is 7? Suddenly, I saw seven knights came to save me. "We are princes from duchies of Brandenburg, Saxony, Frankfurt, Pfalz, Bavaria, Bohemia and Alas. You are saved!"

"Ha-ha! Good bye! Old man! My emperor!" I jumped on a horse and ran away with the princes, leaving a trail of smoke.

V

I intended not only to go further than any man who had been before me, but as far as I think, it is possible for a man to go!

"Capt. James, look!" I shouted. "My role model!!"

"Yes! Brave young man! Join my navigation adventures! We will draw the maps of the New World! Bringing glory to Mankind!"

I rushed to hug him, and I suddenly disappointed.

VI

"Why so FAST!!" I complained. "He is my favorite man!"

"You are beefing badly in the reality. So your time is compressed." Still the voice over my head.

Five fighters were fighting with the enemy, before my eyes. They were fighting the army with the banner of red circle.

Perhaps, they are the warriors of the Lang Ya Mountain. Like what I did in Beijing. I charged at the Japs, with a rifle in my hands…

VII

On the wasteland, I saw four travelers.

A jumping monkey, a dressed pig, a man carrying luggage and a monk.

"Journey to the West." I smiled.

Sun Wukong came to me. "We will be busily crossing the river later. But I can't still save a little time to gift you with ability. What do you want?"

"Turn someone else into animals. Just like you can turn yourself into 72 shapes." I said.

Then I was embraced and I went to the next scene.

VIII

"We are not born on the same day. But we wish to die together!" three men vowed.

"That must be three brothers. Liu Bei, Guan Yu, Zhang Fei!" I thought.

I walked to them and drank a glass of their blood.

"Take me along with you!" I said happily.

IX

I rested for a while.

Then I found a rock to lean against. This scenario was weird. Nothing happened for a long time.

All of a sudden, a young man and a young woman broke out of the windows and jumped from the building.

I ran to check.

Yes, they were Liang Shanbo and Zhu Yingtai.

I didn't dare to look at them.

"Let me turn you into butterflies!" I said to myself as Sun Wukong told me.

Then they flew away. Butterflies' Love!

X

Void and void.

"The last one is you!" said the spirit of nature.

"It represents the '1'."

"I'm ready to die." I said silently.

"Don't be too anxious. Ha-ha. Let me talk."

"An individual human existence should be like a river, small at first, normally contained within its banks and rushing passionately past boulders and waterfalls. Gradually the river grows wider, the banks recede, the water flows more quietly. In the end, without any visible break, they merge in the sea."

"But you, you are a young man, you have love for your nation and care for others. Most importantly, you dare to fight the evil. You have eyes to seek beauty. I link you with life and origins of things. It's as if you teens are, in some sense cosmic beings in violent and lovely contrast with me."

"I grant you a new life."

End Credit

I was on the street again, listening to my favorite *Jasmine Flowers*, I suddenly recalled a song:

Those were such happy times and not so long ago.
How I wondered where they'd gone.
But they are back again.
Just like a long lost friend.
All the…

Yesterday Once More!
With ten young hearts of rising sun!

（作者学校：新疆维吾尔自治区乌鲁木齐市第一中学）
本文为2017年"北大培文杯"决赛参赛文

> **作者的话**
>
> 　　我虽是理科生一枚，但绝对够文艺。钢琴、舞蹈陪伴我走过青葱岁月，英语更是我成长道路上必不可少的甘霖。爱音乐，从艾薇儿到少女时代；爱小说，从周国平到东野圭吾；爱运动，从羽毛球到长跑；爱旅行，从喀纳斯湖到台湾海峡。欣赏别人的创新，但也期待自己能迸发出新颖的灵感。"培文"之旅虽有些许遗憾，却是人生路上一个难得的闪光点。在触碰到梦想之前，我不会停下来，我会一直遵循着心的方向奔跑到未来。
>
> 　　勿忘初心，方得始终。

THE FIRM WALL OF MORA

姚文瑾

I

"Today is our annual conference of reelection. I, the king of MORA Kingdom, will announce the consequence of this formal election." Gin stood on the platform of the castle, reading out the document in front of all his people with applause and excitement.

"… Congratulations, Rye! You will be the earl, and the officer of our fantastic experiment." Everyone shouted and applauded when Rye was pushed to the front. "Welcome to the 'builder' of institution's wall!"

"It's my pleasure, my honorable king." Rye bowed gratefully.

After the celebration, the former officer led Rye to their secret laboratory, introducing the regulations to the new man.

"Be cautious for your words and behavior. Don't attempt to resist the king or refuse his order. Or you will be like this!" The man showed his broken arm, warning Rye at the end of the aisle.

"The door should be opened by you alone. Hope you can retire successfully at this age." The old man patted Rye's shoulder and left.

"What? Isn't it overstated?···um···" Rye muttered and opened the door.

"Welcome to my secret laboratory, Rye." As soon as he pushed the door, a queer feeling blew on his face. Gin had already waited for him, wearing a mysterious smile.

Before he bowed, Gin had held his hand, "Young man, on the next screen you will see the biggest mystery in our Kingdom. Don't be afraid and flee. That's the firm wall of MORA."

Then, Gin pushed the inner door, followed by Rye.

II

There was no light in the final room, but a faint blue light coming from lots of glass containers, which were filled with organs and organized systems in the odd blue liquid.

"What the hell are··· are these?" Rye stunned exceedingly and asked.

"I am attempting to make robots with super organs and cells that can protect our Kingdom and defend the invasion. They will help me conquer the whole world and become the king of the world. Certainly, they will never suffer pain, sadness, even death. Isn't it perfect? With these robots, we won't be terrified by any enemy.

"However— I'm in the procedure. I need your help."

Looking at Rye's shocking face, Gin continued, "I know you may not accept it immediately, but I heard that you are respectable in the people, and you can help bring some dead bodies to me. That's your task."

"That's stupid! To their relatives, how can I account for this? Will they accept this experiment? People have never known it!" Rye refuted excitingly.

"How dare you disobey me? I have done these for twenty years and every officer did it for me without hesitation! You should think how to cope with those silly people yourself, not by asking me! If you refuse… Hmm, I think you are a smart young man." Gin went out and looked askance at Rye.

Rye touched one of the containers mildly and held his fists.

III

Two years passed.

"Well done, Rye! I always believe you are a competent man." Gin watched his new experiment materials gladly, "You are an indispensable assistant on my way to success. I will award you when I receive all of those glories."

Rye looked down on the ground and gnashed the teeth in anger, "It's my pleasure, king."

The days passed tranquilly, Rye had become Gin's believable man. Gin appreciated him utterly, and always discussed the procedure with Rye.

It's February 26th, 309BC. There was a battle held by people in MORA, suddenly.

Gin, the noble king, was in a great rush, giving orders to his languid soldiers to attack the resisting people.

Rye protected Gin and guided him to the laboratory.

"More than grateful, Rye. I must have been dead without you." Gin locked the door and had a temporary rest.

"Oh yes. And you will still die a little while." Rye sneered.

"What are you saying? You⋯" Before Gin finished his words, Rye pushed the sword to his chest hard and pulled out.

Gin fell down and stunned, "You⋯ you are traitor! Damn it!"

"I have been plotting this battle for two years, since you gave me the earl and let me see your experiment. Of course, those materials were not humans— they were from cows, horses and sheep. You must be mad! You took those organs for this immoral experiment, only for your own ambition! I think I haven't told you, my sister is in your glass container! I have told this experiment to your people, and I will bomb this laboratory just a little while. Goodbye, my honorable king."

Without any weapons in hand, Gin spit the blood and roared with laughter, "Traitor! Traitor! Traitor⋯"

Because of the lack of military training, people won the battle readily. They pushed Rye to be their king. Rye's entire nightmare had been over.

IV

It's March 9th, 309BC.

The new-start celebration held in front of the castle.

In order to protect the people from invasion, Rye rebuilt the wall of MORA and strengthened it.

"Rye! Rye! Rye! Rye!" Everyone shouted with excitement to welcome their new pleasurable king.

"It's more than a pleasure to be here. Sorry for keep you waiting for this moment for so long. I had ruined Gin's laboratory and sent back the organs of your relatives. Mourn the dead, and⋯ start a new kingdom!"

"Rye! Rye! Rye! Rye!"

"My name is Rye. Our kingdom is MORA, which is the token of 'moral'. I promise I will bring you a peaceful life."

Now, I declare solemnly:

"The wall of the old institutions has been broken down! And the original MORA Kingdom has been founded!"

（作者学校：新疆维吾尔自治区乌鲁木齐市第一中学）

本文为2016年"北大培文杯"决赛参赛文

Dear Mr. Robot-I

> **作者的话**
>
> "世界永远是新的,无论它的根多么古老。"于我而言,科幻从未止步于作品本身。它是地外智慧,是星际航行,是宇宙与人性碰撞之后孕育的第一声叹息。机器抑或人类,最后都会回归母星的怀抱,成为亿万原子漫长生命中的无数过客。

LOST WITH THE ISLAND

赵君彤

He woke, and remembered dying.

—Ken Macleod

Jeremy woke, and shivered from the feeling of cold and wet. Out there was a dark and cloudy sky.

He managed to stand up, scanned the mind, only to find nothing matching this place. It seemed like he got himself on an island in a totally unknown place.

Soon or later, he saw a palace decorated with wires and flowers, and Jeremy decided to enter. After all, he had nothing to lose, he thought.

When pushing the door, a sense of déjà-vu struck him like a beam of electricity going through his body, made Jeremy stumble and barely hold himself back.

Inside the palace, there was⋯ a tunnel, a tunnel which was lined with memorial exhibits, all frozen in some ice-like solid, shines right beside him.

Jeremy couldn't help but rushed to the nearest— the photo of five astronauts, carrying their helmets, their smile was pure and passionate. It's the Arys— the spacecraft which crashed with an unexpected space trash and none of her staffs survive. Yet here they were, smiling to him through the abyss of death, reminded Jeremy of their stories.

This was not right, Jeremy vaguely thought, how was I supposed to have such a strong feeling of them? I was born far from their era, let alone I was not their descendants.

However, he moved forward. The exhibits included a piece of Mark Twain's manuscript, a fragment of the earliest serving robot KD-5, the application of Dr. Ross appearing throughout his life, but they all aroused Jeremy's affection, like he was a ghost carrying other men's memories. No matter what was happening to him, it was against logic.

The feeling of cold and wet still accompanied him but he was no longer aware of it. He was too immersed in his own thoughts to be aware of anything happening around.

Finally, at the end of all exhibits, he saw a girl. She was no longer a kid, but it was also inappropriate to call her a woman. Her hands held on to someone's for dear life as they were swirling around, the other man's face couldn't be seen for he was at the back of the camera.

Something struck Jeremy right down to his core, something so powerful, so true, that he couldn't tell it was not anyone else's memory, but his— his own memory.

Dear Mr. Robot-I

At that time he felt burning, like sinking in boiling magma, but it made Jeremy notice what was the cold and wet feeling exactly.

It was the feeling of lost.

"It was a pleasure to burn." He murmured, quoted Ray Bradbury, and then let the heat drown him.

"… Doc, it looks like he didn't make it."

"For earth's sake, Sam, stop staying such and have some faith in Jerry!"

He woke, and almost went blind in the gigantic sun. It must be the caution of his feeling of burn. The air around him was thin. Jeremy managed to stand up, and helmet gave a call.

"Thank earth you back into conscious, Jerry. Give us your condition report."

Jeremy heard his own flat voice, "Status stable, no terminate damage, Doc. So far so good."

"Then, congratulations, Jerry. You may proceed, to enterprise this planet."

He followed Diana's words, started walking around on the Mercury, and picked some ashes and dusts waiting to be analyzed. As doing his jobs, Jeremy still had the same feeling when he was in coma. The sense of lost. The sense of something had gone forever from his inside. Diana's voice made it bearable, but the hole in his heart still existed.

"… Jerry, if the mission is accomplished, you will be the first robot to land on the Mercury successfully. The honor belongs with us, the Futurobotics!"

He heard applause right through the communication device.

Jeremy turned it off and flashbacked to that precious picture, which Diana was happily swirling in.

That was the only thing belonging to him, and the only reason why his intellectual system withstood the heat of the sun.

Yes, he IS a robot from Futurobotics Inc., a.k.a JM-5 officially to the public. Jeremy is his nickname. It is Diana who named him according to his number. Dr. Ross is one of the most famous roboticists in the company, and he is Diana's grandfather. He is also Jeremy's father model, JM-2— its owner.

The exhibits he saw in the memory palace, turned out to be his former models' memory.

They all worked for the Ross' family.

And Diana incredibly inherited her grandfather's work and genius, had grown up and began to work for the Futurobotics.

Her grandfather built Jeremy as a precious gift to Diana, for he had emotion sections inside the intellectual system.

However, Diana didn't find out. She thought that was impossible, and the heartwarming feelings from Jerry was just a childhood craze. So as growing, she began to treat him as a robot, like others do.

And yet now he is, standing on the Mercury, alone and feels nothing. Jeremy hopes he could return to that island again, but no. He will never meet these memories again.

He is lost with the island forever.

（作者学校：吉林省长春外国语学校）
本文为2017年"北大培文杯"决赛参赛文

作者的话

最初，只是小心翼翼，字字斟酌，悄悄地把自己藏进文字里。心绪，只对自己言说。培文杯，于我而言，是一个舞台。是它，让我有机会将我心中的小小世界表达，将真实的自我展现。写作，是写他人，亦是写自己。仰望天河，繁星点点，夜色温柔，谁能想到苍穹之外的宇宙竟是无尽的冰冷与荒凉？剥开自我，坦然面对世界。去吧，我始终相信，勇敢的少年会创造奇迹。

感谢培文杯，点缀了我 16 岁的盛夏。

ALICE IN APRIL

孙菡治

The tide rises, the tide falls.
Many legends are told,
Some turn into dust,
Some turn into gold,
History is like wind,
Blowing across the endless river of time⋯

I

April 1st, 3018 A.C.

Survivor of the Future Gazer: 1

I'm the man-made human being— the Future Gazer 10032, you can call me Alice. When I'm writing down this report, it has been 531 years since the human being started the project— Escape the Earth. We the future gazers have carried the duty to search for a new planet for continuing the culture of the Earth. Having wandered in the dark space for several centuries, we find nothing.

Most of the time, I keep asleep into the VR world, for the resource to support my life is limited. In the VR world, I relive the life on the Earth, which the human beings have created and ruined by themselves.

I've seen the first breed of crop sowed to grow up into an amazing culture in Huaxia; I've seen the ancient Greek people found the core values of human beings, liberating the honorable creature from the hands of God; I've seen the glory Ancient Roma Times when the Lord Caesar conquered across the land; I've seen the wheels of the Industrial Revolution started to roll, suggesting the beginning of the decline of the earth culture.

I've seen the butterflies dancing around the vibrant flowers in spring, I've seen the breeze blowing across the beach bathed in the sunshine in summer, I've seen the leaves kissing and saying goodbye to the branches in fall, I've seen the snowflake decorating every Christmas in winter… I've seen the four seasons changed in turns, making up every single year.

Though I'm a man-made life with few self-emotions, I can still feel the tender of spring, and my heart hurts when it comes to the broken earth.

I set the clock to wake me up on April 1st every year. Because I know it is spring now. It's the best season in a year to bring every wonderful dream into reality.

However, what I've seen now is still the dark, cold space. No life, no hope.

By the way, the signal lights of the other future gazers have all been turned off, which suggests the fate of mine— the last child of the Earth, lost in the endless space.

I check my supporting nutrition, which almost runs out. The death is waving to me, I can escape nowhere.

It is my last spring, it is my last April.
April is the cruelest month,
Breeding lilacs out of the dead land,
Mixing memory and desire,
Stirring the dull roots with spring rain ⋯

— *Thomas Eliot*

II

I'm Alice, the Future Gazer 10032. There are 3 hours 5 minutes left in my life. I'm in my spaceship, which is almost out of work.

Out of gravity, blank in my mind, I know I could change nothing. It's April 5th 3018 A.C., when spring should have begun in the Earth.

The programs in my mind have not taught me what is "love". After all, "love" itself is not a word that can be expressed by other words. I'm grateful for the scientists who created me and gave me the name "Alice", which carries sweetness and romantics.

I've navigated in the universe for a long time. It is my duty to search for a new planet to start a new culture of the Earth. There are several containers in my spaceship that carry cells of different creatures on the Earth. Once I land, the machines will start to work, cloning the cells to build a vibrant new world.

However, all the dreams will come to an end.

How could it be like this?

I eventually understand.

Human beings are too self-centered and selfish. They think they could rule the Earth. They think they could change the laws of nature. They destroy the environment for their ambitions. They ruin the motherland which fed them up.

They think they are angles, ironically, they are exactly the devils.

They want to make the world a heaven, however, they are lost on the halfway.

They created me with the hope that they could save everything. It was just too late.

The Earth, she is not your slave, instead, she is your friend.

III

Green eyes reflected in the glass cover and then the black world takes place of everything, just like spring disappears in the dark universe.

I have a dream the first time in my life. I dreamed I were a poet in the grasses. I rode my horse and sang for my life and who I were. I sang for the spring day that gave me hope; I sang for the liveliness in my eyes.

April 5th, 3018 A.C.

Survivor of the Future Gazer: 0

The tide rises, the tide falls.

Many legends are told,

Some turn into dust,

Some turn into gold,

History is like a sign.

Blowing across the endless river of time…

（作者学校：四川省泸州高级中学）

本文为2018年"北大培文杯"决赛参赛文

DO YOU HEAR ME, LITTLE PRINCE?

> ▼ The crisis of today is the joke of tomorrow. For me, every grass is now a green tree, and every white petal of yours is a fragrant flower! Ah, you remind me that I have lost so many things.
>
> ——Hans Christian Andersen

童心者，绝假纯真。童话于儿时的每个人不可或缺，又逐渐与很多人渐行渐远。本节的小作者们秉持着一如既往的稚子初心，带着对世间万物的好奇与喜爱，书写出一篇篇妙趣横生的童话故事。

　　这里有温柔的魔法铃声，有《小王子》中玫瑰花的深情告白，有头上长角的善良"怪兽"，有充满着爱的奇幻"标签"……每一页的想象，都返璞归真，书写着人性的真、善、美。

　　这里也有拟人化视角的童话故事，小作者们用生动的语言、完整的结构为生命发声。不论是在人类文明中艰难求生的小鸟，还是努力奔向自然怀抱的马戏团老虎，所有的生命都渴望回归自然与本性，都期盼在困境中突出重围，实现自我成长。一篇篇童话故事正如同生命之间的对话，是实现这种渴望的力量之源。

　　愿每一个人都能在童话世界中，寻得文学初心。

> **作者的话**
>
> 一个人的行走范围，就是他的全世界。培文杯给了我一个走出来的机会。是的，我走出来了，遇见了最美的蓝天、花海和最美的你们。培文杯给了我更多的梦想和更多的坚持与坚强。有了培文的陪伴，我希望自己能与北大牵手，可以成长为天地间徜徉的雄鹰，朝起夕回，日日沐浴于阳光下、清风中。

DO YOU HEAR ME, LITTLE PRINCE?

宋元煦

The tide rises, the tide falls. That is what moon causes. But the tide in my heart rises and falls, just because of you, my little prince.

— Your rose

Do you hear me, little prince?

I remember the first day I came to your planet, dear little prince, you looked so close to me, guessing if I was a new kind of baobabs. To my astonishment, you didn't try to kill me, but to take care of me instead. Every day you saw me from a sprout to a bush, I could always hear your gentle breath besides me. That always made me smile after you left me.

Do you hear me, little prince?

I acknowledge that sometimes I'm a trouble for you. At first, I was not satisfied to complete my preparations for my beauty in the shelter of chambers all the time. I dressed myself very slowly. I adjusted my "skirt" one by one. Then one morning, exactly after sunrise, I came up and smiled to you. So long for you have waited for me, your blue eyes shone, like the stars around us, only for me.

Do you hear me, little prince?

I'm sorry that my vanity hurts you all the time, and I really misunderstand the meaning of love. I remember that the day I finally came up, I pretended to be sorry and said, "I beg your excuse. I'm not dressed perfectly yet." In fact, I thought I was the greatest flower in universe in my heart. I even said that I was born at the same time of the sun! But you just stood there, praising me: "How beautiful you're!"

I also remember that when I was speaking of my four thorns, I asked you with excitement: "Are there any tigers on your planet? I would scare them with my thorns." You objected: "Tiger didn't eat weeds!" "I'm not a weed! I'm a rose!" I shouted at you. "I'm sorry…" Your voice sounded a little tired. Both of us remained silent, seeing the sun disappear.

Do you hear me, little prince?

I didn't know that the concept of love didn't mean I could do whatever I wanted though the bond between us was strong until you declared that you would travel to other planets. You're the best man in universe, I know. I'm sorry that I often disturb you, performing sweetly to gain your sympathy, and pretending to be fragile to make you sad. I pushed you to water me with pure water. I even pushed you to find a glass cup to protect me from wind. How silly I was at that time! Dear little prince, however, I just tried to make sure you love me.

I'm sorry, I gave you nothing.

Do you hear me, little prince?

You went to many planets, including a planet governed by an emperor, a planet that a businessman living in, and the earth. A cute bird came here every week to tell me everything about you. I learnt that you had gone through a desert, climbed the mountains and made friends with a pilot and a fox. My face turned "redder" when I heard that you met thousands of roses like me in a garden! Feeling ashamed then, I was still proud of you! You're still the unique one in my heart although the chances are that I'm not the only rose in your heart now.

Do you hear me, little prince?

Gone were the days when we sat together to pray after the sunset, shared the secrets from the bottom of your heart and laughed when the volcanos erupted. I often try to find you on the earth whose color is like your pretty eyes, imagining where you are or what you are doing even though ashes had covered the glass. Every time when I'm missing your innocent voice, your golden hair and your gentle breath, my tears often wet my leaves.

Do you hear me, little prince?

Time may wrinkle my skin, but could never wrinkle my soul, and my heart to love you. I will go away soon or later, but love can make both of us alive forever. I feel sorry I know how to love you so late. So dear, let me love you in heaven.

Tide rises, tide falls, just for you, my little prince.

（作者学校：山东省沂源县第一中学）
本文为 2018 年"北大培文杯"决赛参赛文

Do You Hear Me, Little Prince?

> **▌作者的话 ▌**
>
> 　　一茶勺色彩，一小包汤料，添一点快乐，加一抹忧伤。拌一拌，搅一搅，闻闻隐约飘出的奇妙味道。喜欢阅读，喜欢音乐，喜欢画画，喜欢童话般缤纷的颜色，喜欢随时随地胡思乱想。无边无际的想象对我而言，是平淡时光里趣味十足的调剂，是日常生活中不可或缺的构成。这趟漫长旅途才刚开始，我希望不断尝试并取得崭新的进步，祈盼自己的声音以写作的方式被大家听到。期待有朝一日我的故事能被人喜爱和铭记，那将会是非常幸福的事！

THE GOLDEN BELLS

李松晓

　　The last thing Annie Bells ever thought about was stepping into Charlie Wilson's antique store. With a brief glance at that place, people might get the impression that it was only a little white stone house. However, to tell the truth, for kids on Dandelion Street, going there was worse than reciting a long article aloud in class, or being forced to swallow down a bowl of broccoli at dinner. Rumors spread among the neighbors about the imaginary stories of the shop owner who barely came outside, for the curtains were always drawn, making his store look like a mysterious and enchanted castle. At least that was what Annie thought on the way home, as sun rays filtered through the branches, stroking her hair.

Annie's younger brother Peter was waiting for her on the porch. There was a remarkable resemblance between the two siblings: they were both tall and lean, both had tangled brown hair, freckles, a pair of blue eyes and confident expression.

Peter gripped Annie's arm to pull her aside. "You know what? I heard Mom and Dad whispering something about moving. Recently they've been quarreling a lot for Dad being too busy to accompany us."

Annie dropped her backpack, "Yeah, literally."

"But they're supposed to love each other and stay together! You think they're going to divorce or not?" Peter tugged at her sleeves hastily.

"Not that serious, silly." Snapped Annie, "Divorce? Moving? And next week will be Mom's birthday, that's the awkward case."

The atmosphere at the dining table was tense enough to make Annie forget all about the tales of the antique store. Dad left for work afterwards and Mom went shopping, which meant the two children were home alone cuddling by the fireplace. She looked around at the familiar furniture, the wooden chairs, the shelf that once a beautiful music box stood on. Everything in the room suddenly seemed full of emotional feelings. For the first time Annie realized how the idea of moving made her flustered and miserable. When was the last time Dad played baseball with Peter or Mom took them to the River Park? When

Do You Hear Me, Little Prince?

did they last go for a picnic together? Annie couldn't recall. All that clicked in her mind was singing along to an old song, with golden bells ringing and stars flickering.

She took a glimpse of the calendar on which Dad put labels as a reminder, and her eyes widened. "Pete, come and look at this! Friday—that'll be tomorrow, it says 'the antique store', double underlined."

They stared at each other puzzled and felt a bit excited.

"What's Dad gonna have to do there? Hey, we had better go and check!"

"But the Wilson's place?" Wailed Peter, "they say he eats children and summons apparitions with evil magic! We'll just ask Dad."

"So what? C'mon, it may be the only chance we expose some mysteries. You reckon Dad will tell? I'd say no way. These days adults are keeping too many secrets."

Annie had always been a fine audacious young lady who was ready to take adventures and explore the other side of things. What might be the danger if Dad was going? Eventually they set off in the warm evening wind of May. The shop was only two blocks away.

"What shall we do after getting in?" Murmured Peter.

"We ask whether Mr. Bells has made an appointment. It won't take long, okay? Perhaps he's a nice guy. Mom said you couldn't stick labels on someone by judging what you see and hear. It's now or never, the very thing we need to do is conquer our fear."

Together they pushed the heavy stone door open.

Even though prepared, Annie flinched and quivered at the sight of the old man sitting behind the counter in the dim lamplight. He was short and had a long white beard, a hooked nose like an eagle's, fierce black eyes deep as night. She faltered and even squealed a little when she asked the question, while Mr. Wilson studied them motionlessly.

"You must be his kids then, Annie and Peter?" He said in a low voice and led them up the stairways. They followed, hearts pounding hard.

Stunned and startled, they watched him unlock the attic door. Oh goodness, what a spectacular scene there was! On the narrow shelves all over the room laid antique bottles, china vases, silk clothing, fluffy teddy bears and dolls from centuries ago. Some were broken and others were complete. Buttons and mittens stood in a row, orange fire flaming, crystal balls shining. Golden and silver bells rang, chanting a melody.

"You… made all these, Mr. Wilson?" Gasped Annie. Only then did she notice the sly and naughty sparkles behind his dark eyes.

"Call me Charlie, will you? I repair them for customers. They are alive and full of feelings; they love and hate just like human beings. For people who appreciate them and cherish them, they can be labels and symbols of a certain life period. Here's the secret of antique stores: I fix precious things and hand them to proper holders."

Annie took a deep breath to let it sink in, while Peter stared in awe. "Um, Charlie? So, you aren't the creepy old guy who summons ghosts and eats kids at all." Said Peter, which was not the correct thing to say.

To their astonishment, Charlie Wilson laughed, his long beard dancing up and down. "Course not! I don't go out because I'm busy repairing the antiques. As for your father's appointment, it's already accomplished."

He carefully took out a music box from a piece of velvet cloth. Annie inhaled, "Whoa, Peter! That's the one we always sang along with when we were kids. It stopped playing months ago."

A smile slowly spread across the old man's face. "You know that your father asked me to make it years ago as a wedding gift? One week ago, he asked me again to mend it for your mother's birthday present. How gorgeous the couple was when they first came here! They've been my friends and clients ever since."

Annie felt dizzy, delightful and unreal at the same time. So, her parents still loved each other as she'd considered. Dad had tried to make up⋯wedding present! And Mom had been right about not to stick labels to anyone or judge them by the first impression. As Mr. Wilson was actually kind and generous while others thought he was freakily horrible. As the antique shop really was an enchanted castle but not a scary one. As Annie often failed in exams but had sensitive instincts and brilliant brain. As Peter was afraid of many things but once in a while he would be brave enough to step into an unknown place. Maybe nothing was permanent and nothing could be labeled easily. But the music box was certainly a label, an important symbol of their stories, like Dad's note of reminder to keep them from forgetting the golden days. Maybe there was something that never changed.

Mr. Wilson pressed a button and tender music filled the air. Annie and Peter heard the tune and lyrics they'd been longing for. That's the song their Dad wrote for Mom by himself; the song they listened over and over in their childhood. The sound of golden bells ringing, tickling and clicking merrily, and the sound of piano playing:

Woken up by the flickering sun rays,

Knowing clearly, it's a brand-new day.

Feel the summer breeze brush across your braids,

Conveying the message that it is now May.

Outside your window tall branches sway,

Roses blossom, taking my breath away.

Running on the beach, listen to gentle waves;

Padding in the sand, while seagulls chase.

Swim in shallow water, sipping lemonade;

Walk back to the dock, where you lay.

Down the road enchanting the mighty spell,

Ringing, singing, are the golden bells.

No one lives forever and this moment fades,

But something will remain, 'cause it never changed.

Our love and hope do not break,

Tomorrow comes but they'll be the same.

Happily ever after? I guess fairy tales aren't fake.

So just carry on and even if I trip,

With you ready to catch me, I'm not afraid.

Annie could sense the sun, the breeze, raindrops and dandelions floating everywhere. A strong and fiery love embraced her heart as memories arose in the back of her mind. She could see waves rushing to shore, to the river. She could hear the golden bells, and see their sweet home up on the hill. The picture made tears swell in her eyes. She wrapped her arms around Peter as they listened silently.

"It'll be the birthday surprise for your mom." Grinned Charlie, patting their shoulders, "take it home for your dad, since you have come. Be careful, the box is delicate."

They said thank you and waved goodbye. Pushing the door open, they felt the actual summer breeze brushing through their cheeks. Moonlight illuminated the road in front of them. Annie closed her eyes, thinking of labels and antiques and music and the loved ones, wishing to memorize this precious moment that never faded.

The next morning the siblings got up early. They scrambled downstairs hand in hand to meet their parents in the living room.

"We got something for you." Annie said quietly.

"Wait, what?" Exclaimed Dad in surprise, "you took the box from the store? How did you get to know?"

Peter beamed proudly, "thanks to the label you put on the calendar."

"That's quite something. Happy birthday sweetheart, although it's too early. Remember?" Dad rubbed his forehead and handed the box to Mom, blushing a little. Mom was too thrilled to say a word.

"Oh dear, how⋯"

"Our song Golden Bells. It can sing for us now."

The four of them hugged tightly for an especially long minute until Annie held up her head, "Mr. Wilson's such a nice guy. I can't imagine why I believed Julie's story of him eating children."

"And summoning ghosts." Chuckled Peter.

Mom sighed. "I've told you that's not true. You never put labels on anyone by judging their appearance or the rumors about them. You get closer and feel genuinely with your heart. Don't let prejudice and fear of unknown occupy your mind."

"Yes, but this, is surely our label." Annie pointed to the music box, "the symbol of a happy family, loving one another and never being separated."

Peter suddenly pulled back. "What about moving? I don't want to leave here."

"Ah, you mean this." Dad let them take a look, "we were planning to move the furniture to make room for the new piano I've been earning money to buy."

The children cheered, delighted. "Now Mom herself is able to play the song."

"What do you think of inviting Mr. Wilson for dinner tonight?" Mom suggested, "he has been helping us a lot, plus he needs friendship and laughter instead of home alone all day long."

"Awesome. I'll call him. I guess he'd love to come."

"Then the neighbors won't be afraid of him once they get to know him outside the store."

While Dad was busy making his phone call, Mom and the kids looked out of the window. "You know what?" said Mom gently, "I won't say that's the best gift I've ever received, because the very best presents I've had is you."

So off they went down the hill to Dandelion Street, merrily singing the old song of Golden Bells. "No one lives forever and this moment will fade. With you ready to catch me, I'm not afraid…" The sound of golden bells rang and tickled, now as a label and the most important symbol, evaporating into the tender summer wind of May.

（作者学校：中国人民大学附属中学）

本文为 2018 年"北大培文杯"决赛参赛文

> **作者的话**
>
> 在培文的一次短暂旅程,却已让我看过世间至美、人间至情,如同在灯光温柔的夜里,看笔下缓缓绽开一朵迎风颤颤、遇雨曳曳的花,千头万绪,一点满足,难以言表。感谢培文,让我的人生路上多了一点值得珍而重之的小确幸,许多繁花满襟、天风盈袖的愉悦,可以更加坚定地裁纸作衣、折笔为骨、以梦为马,走得无畏无惧。愿我们能够一直清醒,温柔,一尘不染。

DON'T BE CLOSE TO IT

邱渝茜

There was a song spread by little birds in the forest called *Don't Be Close to It*, which told birds a rule should be followed. It could be traced back as early as an old mother bird and her children.

I

My mother was an old bird. On account of her affluent experience, she was so discreet that the most significant words she said was "don't be close to it".

We all object to following her words, particularly my brother.

One day, we found a new kind of fruit in the deep forest, which owned an unprecedentedly beautiful color. Imaging the sweet and wonderful taste it could have, we fell in love with it at the first sight.

"Mother said 'don't eat colorful things!'" my sister said to my brother, who was eager to eat it.

"Mother said, mother said, always 'mother said!'" my brother shouted, "I will prove that mother is wrong!"

He had a bite of that fruit but felt disappointed and unhappy: "I don't like its taste. It's very normal."

Finding my brother look very healthy, undeniably there was a doubt in our hearts that mother was wrong.

II

After my brother's action against mother's words, my sister who was interested in city life made a decision to accomplish her dream.

The night before her leaving, we sat by a famous spring in the forest singing a number of songs, enjoying the last happy time.

As a result of the long distance between us in the future, I was concerned about my sister's safety and said: "why do you want to go to the city? Mother always let us not be close to the city."

My sister was filled with vitality and motivation: "Evidently mother shouldn't be right all the time. My friend displayed the difference of city. Not only do they have various plants, but also full of intoxicating things we never have known."

The last sentence she said to me was: "We all think highly of mother's words, but mother should not be absorbed in her boring old times."

A week later, a bird coming back from the city gave me a leaf letter written by my sister. On it, my sister showed me many remarkable things I have just heard in the stories. Besides, she engaged herself in having a fun time in the city and scheduled a tour to more places.

These phenomena enabled me to ask for the truth: "Who is right? Mother or my sister?"

I had a crazy idea.

III

It was the third day I found this person.

"Don't be close to those people easily." It was the most important rule that we needed to obey. I would fight against it.

In my view, he was a kind and friendly man, who always gave birds some delicious food.

I sang songs so as to attract his attention. He found and praised: "What a beautiful bird!"

On his face was a satisfied smile: "Come here and I will give you tasty fruit!"

I encouraged myself to try my best not to be afraid of him. Thanks to my courage, we played together happily.

With unparalleled passion and happiness, we became friends. Because of my trust, he invited me to his house. I was so relaxed that I fell asleep. When I woke up, I found myself kept in a cage astonishingly.

There was an undeniable and inevitable fact that the man caught me! He cultivated the trust of birds and took advantage of it to catch us!

Crying sadly and hopelessly, I found that mother was right! But I couldn't meet her forever! More importantly, when I stayed in the cage, my friends asked the wind to tell me two news. One was my brother died two days ago and the killer was that fruit which contained poison. The other was that my sister disappeared after thrown by a stone, which came from a bad boy.

We all broke the rules and we all got the punishment. Mother was right.

Don't be close to colorful things. Don't be close to cities. Don't be close to people easily. They don't mean barriers.

Like the labels on the goods which expressed the companies' power and confidence, mothers' don'ts was the label of her love and care.

At last, luckily, I was saved by bird-lovers and I came back to the forest.

Every time when I found naive little birds were going to object to his parents' right decision, I would tell them the story about myself.

When I heard the song *Don't be close to it*, I was touched and not able to control my emotion.

The song was the label of sad experience and new future. What the song wanted to sell and tell were the love and care which were deepest and widest.

（作者学校：重庆市巴蜀中学）

本文为2018年"北大培文杯"决赛参赛文

> **作者的话**
>
> "Literature is the fruit of thinking souls." Carlyle once said.
>
> 用一种具有异国风情却又普识的语言来表达心中所想，更是一个令人愉悦的过程。纵使再高明的译者，也无法将一个人内心的所想完整地表述出来。对文学的亲近，便是将此种不可能变为书页翻动后、笔书写后的顿悟与舒畅。跳出了考试的约束，以每一个意蕴深远的词汇去碰撞心中所想，感受到文句如破冰的春水般缓缓而行，充满着重生后的欣喜与雀跃。时代造就了思考，笔下的文字也组成了思想激烈碰撞下小小的火花。也许，在每一篇略显笨拙的文章背后，正是自己想要倾诉于时代的话语。

WHO ARE YOU?

刘雪晗

His world was different from others. Born with a talented gift, the world in his eyes was black or white, except for colorful labels hovering over everyone he met. None of his senses could give him a precise description of one item or someone, as a result of which, reading labels became the only way to build up his world of thoughts. Labels were his most "devoted" friends.

Do You Hear Me, Little Prince?

When he was a naive boy, who was enjoying his time playing with friends in sands, he was kind of those with various labels. Those small squares over children's heads were pink, grass-green or just like the sky color, brushed by a storm.

The boy was fascinated by this pure feeling, during which he learned the desires to sing, to feel, to have fun and to free his heart and soul.

However, as time went by, he also found a few dark labels with cloudy backgrounds. The girl dressed up in a princess suit, was thinking about how to embarrass the most attractive one in their class. Such kinds of labels freaked Freddy out, totally.

Freddy couldn't imagine why there was a dark heart hidden under a glorious dress, with sugary words coming out of cute mouth. He yelled at the dark label and cried "Go away!" but received no response. His heart was so depressed since he couldn't stand evil and dirty thoughts filling in his monotonous life.

Then, Freddy grew up, together with summer dancing pass and winter pacing by. More labels found him.

It was just an ordinary afternoon with rainy clouds. He just arrived home after relaxing himself on the basketball ground. There came the saddest scene: for the first time, he had seen a label named "jealous" firmly attached to his father. With no word left, Freddy silently followed his father and saw a passage jump to his phone's screen. All of a sudden, Freddy realized the whole story about his father's promotion as well as the fake message made to attack the other competitor.

Freddy couldn't believe his own eyes and wished it was just a mistaken message. Still, not until midnight did he fall asleep with doubt and uncertainty.

After all, it was his father! The man he modeled after was a jealous and mean person! But, he is also the one who took dirty measures for winning his promotion. Freddy had never hated his gift like now.

During his time with labels, Freddy came to know that the labels were created by its owners' personalities or by thoughts in others' minds. He disliked the latter one, using which the world became a label cage. Others' opinions just surrounded everyone like ugly fences, and prevented anyone in it from escaping.

Freddy liked Chinese poets, expressing their disagreements on the latter labels attached to them. The poets said that they were just to share the joy of appreciating the moon and drinking with friends, and they enjoyed themselves wandering among maple trees. But the scholars always thought they were used to express sad feelings. Freddy laughed out loudly, though he felt truly sorry for these misunderstanding. Then, it suddenly occurred to him that "Who was not misunderstood?"

Freddy had spent his whole life on deeply digging. He eagerly chased for a pure smile he saw when he was little, the one touched him gently, but often ended up chasing with disappointment.

Just one day before he was leaving for another country, there stood an elderly lady smelling the roses in his backyard.

To Freddy's surprise, no label was hovering over her.

Curiosity drove Freddy come closer and just at the moment she looked up, he was thrilled to find the pure smile! The elderly lady was not in expensive clothes, nor did she wear delicate jewelry. Instead, she was in shabby and dragged a pack of empty bottles. After seeing him, she acknowledged Freddy for his kindness of sharing these charming roses with passers-by and left, smiling contently.

"Who are you?" Freddy asked soundly. "I am just... myself." She just ignored the pity looks around her and moved on to find another empty bottle, leaving Freddy wondering alone.

"We can't forbid others attaching labels to us, but what we have done results in what label we will get." Freddy sank into the sofa, saying to himself. "After all, we are the owners of our labels." Just at this moment, his world went back to a colorful one, and Freddy finally knew the beauty of truth.

And all the labels had gone.

This world doesn't need a label printer or judge. We just need to play our roles well. There do exist persons who are always willing to use a label cage to "distinguish" themselves from others or to "know" people around them. But, nobody has the right to judge someone's life just because the latter doesn't always perform as you expect, let alone use "moral rules" to judge right or wrong.

Everyone is born equal and unique. We are the leading roles who define ourselves. So, don't let the label cage catch you!

（作者学校：山东省昌乐二中）

本文为2018年"北大培文杯"决赛参赛文

| 作者的话 |

你生而有翼，为何竟愿一生匍匐前进，形如虫蚁？

——贾拉尔·阿德丁·鲁米

熊勉之，一个介于潇洒与傲娇之间的十六岁女生。散漫的生活习惯，加上与之极不相称的超强胜负欲，造就了如此平凡却与众不同的我。闲时沉浸在小说架构的世界中无法自拔，又对英语小文情有独钟。日前正品读《老人与海》，肆意感受那波涛汹涌的大海。英语阅读于我，是一个与大洋彼岸相交流、沟通的渠道，同时更是一扇轩窗，供我领略外头的精彩纷呈。

THE YARD BESIEGED

熊勉之

"Edward! Could you please be quiet for a while? I want to sleep!" I scolded him impatiently. I was a tiger, born five months ago, loving sleeping. That was my younger brother, who was full of energy every day. To tell the truth, I did not know why he was so active.

"Thank God. He has left." I let out a long sigh in relief. After a short time, I fell in sound sleep again. Out of my expectation, this time

Do You Hear Me, Little Prince?

I slept for too long to notice someone had brought me away.

When I finally woke, I found that I was in a big yard rounded by a wall. "Mom?" I roared as loudly as I could. Not gaining the reply, I had been attracted by lots of delicious food placed in corner. With surprise and happiness, I threw myself into it and ate delightedly.

"Here is much better than forest, I won't be hungry anymore!" As I was immersed in this surprise, a strong man with a tanned face approached me. It was my instinct that made me draw back. But he only touched my head and stepped back, wearing a light smile.

"I must be the luckiest tiger in the world!" I had been thinking like that every day since living in the yard. One day, a bird landed on the wall and disturbed my sleep. When I was about to be angry, she let out a piercing scream.

"Look! It is a tiger!"

Of course I knew I am a tiger. "Hey, where are your parents?" She asked me and showed a malicious joy. "Is here a wonderful place?" She continued to say. "Yes. The yard is the best home for me." I answered.

I had food, a comfortable bed and a warm home. was there any reason for me to complain about? "Do you still remember the forest? Your siblings are living there. Birds are singing in tune and horses are running around. Maple leaves are rustling gently in the breeze. Oh, how beautiful the scenery is!"

Her description brought me back to my former life. The memory hit me in a sudden. I looked around and wondered if there was a door or a big hole for me to flee out. The iron gate was locked tightly and no hole was here. I bumped against the wall again and again. I didn't escape from here even after the sun had hidden behind mountains.

The next day, I was still dumping it. But I failed, the wall was too hard. "Maybe I won't leave here." I thought.

The man having left for three days came back. Seeing me lay on bed and injured, he came to my aid and bought me many medicines. His actions were very mild, which cut down my pain.

Then he stood by my side and said gently, "Trust me, big cat, you will be better soon. Have a good sleep now." Enjoying his taps on my head, I fell asleep. My eyes were brimming with grateful tears.

Eight years zipping by, I had grown into an enormous and strong tiger. If I kicked a tree, I dared to say it would crack. The wall was still here and I still wouldn't step out. A familiar voice occurred to me. I tried to remember when and where I ever heard it.

My mom! It was my mom!

Eight years passing by, I rushed to the wall again. However, I stopped when I was two meters away from the wall, I was scared. The scars and hurts had disappeared on my body for a long time, but they were in my heart. "I can't! I can't!" I growled in endless pain.

Three days later, a cat climbed up the tree outside the yard. I gazed at him and waited for his words.

"You are a forest king, you should know. The voice let out three days ago was yours, right? I have been looking for you for eight years, how can you sleep here without a sense of shame?"

Words failed me after I listened to her.

"You can make it! You have been strong enough. It is not the wall locking this yard but your heart full of fear that makes you

Do You Hear Me, Little Prince?

hesitate. Come on, you are no longer the small tiger! That poacher is approaching. He is not a good man, he wants your leather!"

What's that? Sometimes in the man's house there were some strange sounds, which frightened me for no reason. If the cat didn't lie to me, it must be a knife!

I turned my head and saw the man walking to me. Hiding his hands behind his back, he walked so slowly. Not until the knife reflected the sunlight did I eventually wake up to reality.

I bumped against the wall.

The wall was not only in sight, but also in my dusty heart.

Along with a big bang, the wall had been broken down. I dashed to the forest I had left for too long and I didn't look back even for once.

I was free.

（作者学校：湖南省长沙市明德中学）

本文为2016年"北大培文杯"决赛参赛文

| 作者的话 |

　　生活是一方包容万千的墨砚，我们则是静候其旁研墨执笔的书生。纵情挥墨，再现生活。一花一木、一叹一咏，皆可入文。正是写作，让我有了洞察万物的兴趣。生活是写作的源泉，创新是写作的动力。创新式的写作不仅能锻炼我们的思维，而且能培养我们多角度思考的能力，而创新的灵感要靠勤奋来获得。越努力越幸运，越创新越成功；让写作融入生活，让生活启迪写作。God helps those who help themselves.

WHO IS THE MONSTER?

曾曼

　　I was a monster— Everyone in my village said so. However, I had no idea that why they all damned me.

　　As soon as they saw me, they threw stones to hit on my body and screamed: "He is coming! Hurry up and beat him…" In fact, I thought I was only a normal person who had strange horns on head. Homelessness, hunger and loneliness were all my feelings for living in such a world which never left me any space to live.

　　Eventually, I was sent to a forest on account of the villagers' decision. Water was absent in the boundary of the forest. Although, they abandoned me and was eager to kill me, I would try to live on my own to the best of my ability.

As entering the center of the forest, I found something amazing—there was a village in the dangerous forest. I was thirsty for food and water, but I hesitated to get close to it.

A voice from the bottom of my heart said: "You are a monster who is ugly and everybody who meets you is alarmed…"

On the contrary, another voice rose in my mind, "Just try it! Nothing is impossible if you try your best to do it."

When I made up my mind to have a try, a tall man opened the door and saw me. I was surprised that he also had horns on his head. For me, it was just like that there was calm after storms.

The tall man looked happy as well. He invited me to have a big meal with his family. How kind of him to treat me! We had a long communication after dinner. According to his words, I knew that I was not a monster but a common person. The people in this village all had horns just like me.

Afterwards, I began to live in the village, which gave me a warm hug and helped me get out of the bad situation. I got acquaintance with the village bit by bit. However, something horrible happened and made me extremely crazy.

That was a sunny day. I decided to play outside. There was a beautiful garden and some fresh vegetables. I had a wonderful time there and didn't get back until midnight. From the far view, I discovered that a big fire was set up in my new village. I dashed to my village with curiosity. However, when I arrived, I saw the cruel view.

Words failed me. They were eating people!

They were monsters— I fell down and couldn't believe my eyes.

The next morning, I came to life in the tall man's home. The man asked why I fell down, I was scared and said nothing. Just now, the man looked like a devil. To escape from the place where I ever had sweet memory, I decided to leave at night. At night, I managed to get out of the forest. But I didn't know where to go and where I could go. On my way, I met a girl who had big eyes and a small face. She was cute and kind. She told me that she had no relatives and earned living here by selling flowers. We became friends soon. Every morning, we picked flowers together. Every evening, we played and made flower baskets. I often asked her whether my horns were ugly and terrible. She always burst into laughing and said: "I never judge by appearances, and you are not ugly at all."

"But in my past village, everyone thought me of a monster, and in my new village, they are the same as me. However, they are monsters!" I couldn't help crying. A gentle touch warmed me immediately and her sweet smile was beautiful, which I would treasure in my mind forever.

"As a matter of fact, true monster lives in people's hearts. Although you are the same as the people who are monsters, you are a good person." She said with smile.

So, who is the monster? I don't know, and I don't want to know. Though, I saw my girl hide something bad. Maybe, she is just the monster or I am the monster. It doesn't matter!

（作者学校：湖南省汉寿县第一中学）
本文为2018年"北大培文杯"决赛参赛文

Do You Hear Me, Little Prince?

> **作者的话**
>
> 你我曾以为这个故事是关于希望、自由与成长,但直到盖上笔帽的刹那,我才发现它就是我对自己人生的承诺。感谢培文杯给了我这个把脑中的奇思妙想化为文字的机会,从此,英文于我不再是一门学科,而是生动鲜活的语言,是可以承载思想的艺术。

DON'T LOSE YOUR LABEL

刘佳淇

Robert had been working on his new comics day and night. This morning he carried his comics, with renewal hope, headed toward his firm: he felt one hundred percent confident, however, his boss's reaction was like a flood of cold icy water spilling all over him. "I'm sorry, Robert. You see, your creation cannot fit the trend well…" Robert couldn't hear the following words clearly, "this must be the 1000th time I've been turned down." Feeling frustrated and desperate, Robert thought to himself.

That night he was going to meet his girlfriend at a luxurious restaurant that served delicious cuisine. But he had to call the restaurant and cancel the reservation, then, see Jenny, his alluring girl, in KFC.

"Hey, Jenny, I apologize for ruining our anniversary, but my work isn't going well, I have to save money for our house, so⋯" "Shh," Jenny put her index finger in front of his lips, smiling apprehensively, "I got it. You know, actually I prefer hamburgers." Robert forced himself to fake a smile, "I'm self-conscious⋯" "Don't be," Jenny grinned at him, "I'll always stand by your side." Robert could not suppress his impulse to kiss her.

Later that night, Robert was busy drawing his new comics, tried to convert them into a more fashionable style. But he couldn't help thinking his last piece. Outrage was burning inside his chest, making him fidget. Eventually he tore his comics into pieces, "I've devoted myself to the comics, but no one⋯ No one ever appreciate that, maybe I should just quit!" "Don't," a remote, mysterious sound appeared. "Who's that?" cried Robert alarmingly, there was supposed to be no one else in the room. "I'm your shadow." The owner of the sound showed up. Robert stared right into his eyes, those eyes were deep, reflective, like the dark surface of a peaceful lake. Robert found himself frozen and unmovable. "For God's sake, you look exactly like me!" "That's for sure, because I'm your shadow. And by the way, my name is Trebor." Robert exhaled gingerly, "How on earth can that happen! Then⋯ why are you here?" "To help you, my master, to be successful." "What?" "Isn't that what you want?" "Of course, it is!" said Robert earnestly. Trebor then grabbed Robert's pen and started to draw. Robert opened his mouth in an O-shape. Trebor's drawing was incredibly attractive. "Please, please draw for me!" "Yes, my master!" answered Trebor obediently.

Do You Hear Me, Little Prince?

Trebor drew like a machine, regardless of tiredness. He completed the comics in one night. The next day, when Robert brought his shadow's work to his firm, he received countless complimentary comments. He never felt that great. He signed lots of contracts and commanded his loyal, hard-working, and most importantly, talented shadow, to finish all of the work. And what's about him? He was going to enjoy his perfect life.

After a month of total recreation, Robert felt something wrong. Sure, life was blissful, but he got an unusual feeling of "not real". He always felt that he was floating in a river toward an unknown barren landscape. Also, his scar on his left cheekbone had almost gone. Robert remembered, in his childhood he hated the scar so much for making him look different from others. His mother comforted him, "my little boy, look, the scar is the label making you unique. Everyone has the label that makes him different from others. You should be proud of that." Robert didn't believe it anymore, that only happened in fairy tales. Now that the scar was disappearing, he was definitely looking more and more handsome.

One night, Jenny came and asked Robert for dinner. But recently Robert was so addicted to a computer game, so he indifferently let Trebor to accompany his girlfriend. After all, they looked exactly the same, who could tell the difference? That night, Trebor was well-behaved, both Jenny and Robert were satisfied. From then on, Robert let out more and more opportunities for Trebor to take over his annoying affairs. Until one day…

"Jenny, come here!" Robert beckoned to his girl, ready for a hug. But there's no response. Jenny was right in front of him, but she couldn't hear him nor see him. "Jenny!" shouted Robert desperately. Silence. Jenny turned around. Then came Robert's shadow, Trebor hugged her and kissed her. Robert went handicapped, he stepped forward to yank Trebor, but suddenly, he found himself transparent, yes, he no longer existed.

At the last minute of his becoming completely invisible, he recalled something his mother had said: "What you do makes who you are, be responsible for your unique label, for your unique soul." Robert staggered up and saw a clear scar on Trebor's— no, actually now— Robert's left cheekbone, "that's his label now." Murmured the disappearing Robert, "the label that used to be mine." The disappearing Robert clenched his fist, reproachfully, disappeared, as if water dropped into a river flowing toward an unknown barren landscape.

（作者学校：北京市第八中学）
本文为2018年"北大培文杯"决赛参赛文

Do You Hear Me, Little Prince?

> **作者的话**
>
> 文学来源于生活，好的文学作品具有一定的现实意义。对我来说，文学是记录现实、感悟现实的工具，让我时时刻刻保持一份"生活的实感"。我写的故事中出现的那一位"average Joe"，又何尝不是我们之中许多人的写照呢？在文学作品中，我体会到了不一样的生活，丰富了自己的阅历。文学让我具有了脚踏实地的充实感。这就是文学对于我的意义。

A LABEL OF STATUS

李正锴

Once there was an ordinary worker named Stones. He worked hard but only got low salaries. He had a family of three, including his wife and son. One day when he was walking along the street, he saw some rich men get off their cars and go into a luxury hotel. "Look at all the things they have got!" Stones thought, "How I wish I could get the statues like them!"

Since then, Stones began to pray all the time, hoping the god would give him an opportunity to change his statues. One day when he was working, something flew swiftly and dashed right into his pocket.

"What the hell is this?" he asked in puzzle. It appeared to be a blank label. "Damn it, who needs a label? But I can write my name on it and put it on my bag and so on." Thinking so, he wrote his name on the label and put it in his pocket without more concern.

After a while, the boss came to see whether all the workers worked well. When he came to the place where Stones was in charge, he strangely got extreme angry. "Stones! Where are you! You lazy guy!" Stones could not believe his ears as he was standing right before his boss, but the boss considered him as air. "Sir I…" Stones wanted to say something but the boss still seemed not noticing him. "I'm wondering why there are so many stones on the floor, maybe I should ask the cleaner to sweep the floor." The boss muttered to himself. Stones thought he must have been crazy as the floor was clean and tidy and there was no stone at all. Feeling scared, stones ran out of the office, only to hear the scream around him. "Loooooook! Small stones are rolling by themselves!" Everyone around him was puzzled. Stones suddenly realized that the workmates had treated him as a real stone! In chaos he took off his jacket and got back to find out the reason. The colleagues finally recognized him and said "Oh, where have you gone?" "Did you see the tiny stones rolling everywhere? But now they have disappeared all of a sudden."

Stones got highly confused and exhausted that night. He put his hand into the pocket of his jacket and the label was found. "Does the label have the magic to change the owner's status?" Stones then changed the name on it and wrote "snake" on it. When he got out the room with the label in his hand, his wife and son cried out loudly and rushed out as fast as possible.

"Ha-ha! Now I can transform my status with any limits, now I will let everyone respect me!" Stones laughed with satisfaction. He wrote "the most handsome man on earth" on the label and walked in the street, finding that everyone's sight was focused on him. When he went into the hotel with "boss of the giant enterprise", the waiters gave him the best service. By making full use of the label of statues, he got many things that he could not have experienced before.

Happy though, the problems came out. Though Stones could change his status freely, he didn't have the capability referring to the status. He wrote "wise man" on the label so there came a large amount of persons who wanted to learn more. But that was what Stones lacked. Though he could become the richest individual, he still got low salaries from his company. Every time he changed his status into elites, he only got instant happiness and joy, then he had to go back to his normal life for the lack of knowledge, wealth or ability, he became an average Joe as usual.

It's not sad to be an average Joe, but sad to be an ordinary guy after being wealthy. Making comparisons between the normal life and luxury status, Stones luckily found his way. He chose to be an ordinary guy but still learn new things. He still worked hard but began to make progress day by day. He still got low salaries but started to really enjoy his life. He tried to love his status and became a firm part of the city, the society and the country. And the label? It was thrown into the rubbish bin, waiting for the next stupid guy who just wanted to change his status.

Status is not only reflected by the labels, but also by our capability, our depth in mind, our wealth both in hand and mind. So, the best status is not the most luxury one, it is the status we really deserve. If you want to go higher, then use your own mind and walk by yourself. Remember that status itself is not important: it is what the status reflects that counts.

（作者学校：湖南省怀化市第三中学）
本文为 2018 年"北大培文杯"决赛参赛文

Do You Hear Me, Little Prince?

> **作者的话**
>
> 平时埋首于针对高考英语的正规学习，成天背诵着"生僻词汇"和"高级句型"，创意作文于我来说，是心上一抹"白月光"——可望而不可即，直到2018年我遇见了"北大培文杯"英语创意写作大赛。初赛时，我用自己对时代的观察和切身的体会来回答 What do young people worry about? 复赛时，我正好阅读了英文版的《小王子》，凭借延伸的想象，构思出我与 Cartoon Character 之间的奇妙旅程。决赛在炎夏北京赛场上，我将平时对 Label 的诸多思考和见闻诉诸笔端，创造了一个"标签"的奇幻世界。我想，创意写作要求的绝不是生僻词汇和繁杂堆砌的句型，我更喜欢用最地道的表达将想象与写实有机结合，并以文学的方式对现实做出隐喻。其实，那抹"白月光"触手可及。

FREE FROM LABELS

吴一婕

"You are the person whom you choose to be, not the one in other's eyes."

My name is May Day. Actually, it is what everyone calls me since my birthday fell on the 1st of May.

I live in a small planet where everyone knows about each other clearly. There is an enormous but perfect system running the planet, making it "peaceful and harmonious" according to our law.

Every citizen on our planet has his own labels, floating above his head and accompanying him like a shadow. Some labels are one's basic information like name, age and address, while others are about one's characteristics, hobbies and experiences.[1] For example, if you have a "brave" label, you can't be afraid of any challenge; if you have a "stupid" label, you won't be admitted into any university in order to save resources for smarter people. However, if you have done something "bad", your labels will keep you out of any public places like schools, libraries and even markets.

I have been accustomed to the world for 17 years. Everyone here is always living cautiously to live up to his labels and so am I. One of my labels is "quiet", in which case I must contain my inborn explosive energy. I always hang out with my friend Charlotte secretly.

One day, we met a strange man in the woods, a person without labels! We were so astonished and a little curious. Charlotte persuaded me to go home, but looking into the man's sincere and shy smile. I decided to talk to him.

"Hi, I am May Day." I extended an oliver branch to him.

"Hi, I am Mike, an adventurer from the Earth. My spacecraft has broken. Oh, what's that? Labels?"

"Everyone has their labels here. As you see, I have mine, too." I

---

[1] Some labels are distributed at random while others are added later during one's lifetime.

let out a sigh. The man looked through my labels, "Kind, academic, shy and quite⋯"

"No! No! That's not me! I don't wanna be like that! Someone asks me to! I hate them all!"

Seeing my annoyance, the man quickly apologized to me. "Sorry, sorry to misunderstand you. Maybe you can change yourself." With his encouragement, great passion starts in my body.

Soon we became good friends. I went to visit him frequently and every time I have problems. His wise words were like a bunch of light, directing me the way of my life. I enjoyed the time when he told me the stories on earth, a world without labels, developing my desire to travel to the earth.

However, our secret appointment was let out by Charlotte, my best friend. She uncovered the whole thing to the police: May Day visited an alien without labels frequently.

Regardless of the anger of teachers and parents, I ran as fast as I could to Mike's place. But it was too late: there was only a note on the table, reading "Your world doesn't agree with me. Without labels, I will never be admitted to true society. But free in nature as I am, I can't put myself under labels. Remember that, my friend, you are the person who you choose to be, not the one in others' eyes. Live in the way you choose for yourself!"

Tears welling up my eyes, I am the one who I choose to be! I am bound to commit my whole being to save myself, to save my world! I held my fists firmly.

I went to the schools, where students with the "stupid" and "lazy" labels were shouted at by their teachers. No one was willing to play with them. They were trapped in themselves, convincing that they were stupid kids by nature.

I went to the prisons, where prisoners with the "theft" and "robber" labels were abandoned by the society and abandoned themselves to despair. They convinced themselves bad guys.

In ever places in my world, all think they are what the labels decide. Everyone gets used to their labels, locking themselves in labels and unwilling to make any positive changes. They just do what the world asks them to do and as a result, living a "peaceful" life, refusing to follow their hearts. What's worse, sincere and explicit communication is abandoned due to the "clear" labels.

Maybe the world doesn't need labels. I told them.

Let's get rid of labels!

People raised their heads, with some light in their eyes, which in my eyes, was more beautiful than the lightest star in the sky. It was what they were. I smiled with satisfaction. Everyone is a star in the sky, shining in different ways.

Free from labels and enjoy what you are. After all, "You are the person who you choose to be, not the one in other's eyes."

（作者学校：江苏省宜兴中学）

本文为 2018 年"北大培文杯"决赛参赛文

作者的话

一茶勺色彩，一小包汤料，添一点快乐，加一抹忧伤。拌一拌，搅一搅，闻闻隐约飘出的奇妙味道。喜欢阅读，喜欢音乐，喜欢画画，喜欢童话般缤纷的颜色，喜欢随时随地胡思乱想。无边无际的想象对我而言，是平淡时光里趣味十足的调剂，是日常生活中不可或缺的重要构成。这趟漫长旅途才刚开始，我希望不断尝试并取得崭新的进步，祈盼自己的声音以写作的方式让大家听到。期待有朝一日我的故事能被人喜爱和铭记，那将会是非常幸福的事！

TO THE SKYLINE

李松晓

It was a dull, misty morning, shades of gray softened the edges of the horizon. I hovered over the waves, taking deep breaths of the salty wind.

A quick glimpse of the sea, I saw that boat. Standing on the deck was a young man sailing on his own. I dived down, landed and said hello.

"Hey buddy." He laughed without surprise, seeming enjoying a companion for a talking bird. "Where are you going?" I asked curiously.

"A mysterious island lives a lady. She has long golden hair gleaming as sun glows, a pair of attractive eyes like dazzling pools. She sings the most enchanting songs in the world. I'll seek for her and make her my bride." he leaned towards me so that I could get a look. There was an old map and one portrait of a glamorous maiden.

I was impressed. It was obvious that he was an interesting guy. I stayed on the board for the rest of the day chattering to the boy, for I couldn't think of anywhere else to go. He kept turning the wheel, seemed to be confused.

He sat down in disappointment as night fell. "We probably lost. We can't push through the fog. I'm afraid."

"Don't be," I comforted him, "you still get to search for your future bride."

"True. But I'm afraid of the darkness, which makes me lose all sense of direction."

"Yet that's only because you don't see the starlight. Somewhere through the mist it's flickering. I see it often while flying across the ocean."

I tried my best to persuade him but he put his face in his hands. "Too much," he mumbled, "too hard. It's been so many days like this that I can't bear it."

"Then why did you have the courage to set sail alone?"

He sighed, "I had to find the girl in my dreams. The fellows back home insisted I must be crazy to chase after an illusory tale. Nobody even believed me at all. I've chosen a path different from anyone else.

Now I'm afraid because I don't have a single friend. What if they're right and I'm wrong? What if the lady isn't the way I thought she might be? This could lead to nowhere."

Excellent. All of his worries were bursting out today. I asked softly, "That's it? Your bewilderment?"

"Still, I'm afraid of what's waiting ahead, of thunder and lightning, of others making fun of me, of the fierce pirates who could've robbed my necessities. I'm afraid of being unusual or ordinary and plain like common people. I have come to pursue my happiness and prove my strength, but I'm afraid of myself one day becoming bored and tired, wanting to turn around, and forgetting what I've been longing for. I'm such a coward."

"Would you rather give up then?" I demanded.

The boy slowly shook his head, expression firm and eyes bright. "I won't go back until I come to that lady's side. Even though I'm afraid, even if I'm lost, I shall keep sailing until I reach the faraway skyline."

Suddenly I was jealous of him. Though I was rarely scared of anything or meditated that much, I perhaps never made any decisions as unflinchingly as he did. I wasn't sure who I might seek or where I should leave for. "You actually don't need to consider so many possibilities. See, I'm a young seagull too, standing out from the crowd who eat and sleep and hide for the rainstorms all day. I wanted to be unique so I flew away, but didn't know where to go. You're brilliant because you have passion, determination and purpose.

"Never call yourself a coward. Leastways you behave far better than those who can't make any choices. You are extremely brave because you aren't afraid to admit your fear."

He looked up, definitely shocked by my comment. "You think so?"

"Yeah. Ever heard this lullaby? I learned it from other sailors."

Stars glow above us in the sky,
Like some shiny jewels that can fly.
Drop all of your fear and extra worries,
The moonbeam illuminates the path by your side.
Let us make sail and set off right now,
If the ocean is peaceful and calm tonight.
The ship to another shore awaits in the harbor;
Until the morning sun sparkles in your eyes.

I recited the lyrics. He quietly sang along. The mist was dissipated now, as we could catch sight of tiny twinkling rays of light.

"Thanks." the boy whispered, "I've been quite lonely for a while, but I got your support now."

And it hit me in one split second. Just like him, I could head forward to the distant skyline. I'd take risks. I'd explore. I would be going on and on. With the goal set in my heart and the melody echoed in my mind I wouldn't easily get drown. One day I must find a way out.

Silently I sent a wish upon the stars. Please give us power and strength to get there. Please let us find our direction. Please make us tough and firm and confident.

Do You Hear Me, Little Prince?

Firm enough to meet our final ends. Tough enough to stand and fight. We got hope, enthusiasm and courage. We could transform darkness into light.

At dawn, we waved each other goodbye, and then went our separate ways. His head held up high, facing the blue sky.

I spread my wings and flew, nowadays I'm still flying. To the far-off horizon. To the hazy unknown destination. Across thunderstorms and hurricanes. Survived through the pirates and fishing nets. Until I reach there I won't fall. With this belief I could be strong. With this faith each morning is brand new. Because that's what he does, although I haven't met him since then, I always know. Maybe the ending of the story isn't important any more.

I didn't ever look back.

And I shall never regret.

（作者学校：中国人民大学附属中学）
本文为2018年"北大培文杯"复赛参赛文

> **作者的话**
>
> 双鱼座，爱好读书、音乐、摄影和乒乓球，曾任石家庄一中星水文学社副社长，发表过多篇作品。在第四届、第五届"北大培文杯"青少年创意写作大赛全国总决赛中分别获得二等奖和一等奖。喜欢在题海中苦苦遨游的间隙，伸手在创意的天空，描绘心灵的影像，写下成长的感悟，采撷人间的美好。感谢文字，让滚烫的情绪在心底最柔软的地方炼化出鲜活而又淋漓的感动，帮助我坚持唤醒沉睡的耳朵，捕捉世间最纯粹的音符，谱写出纸上灵动的乐章。

THE LABEL OF LOVE

王逸菲

Everyone seems to be born with something. Some are born with high IQ, some are born with talents for music, and some are born leaders. However, Eric found his father Liam a born rock. Liam, a chemistry teacher, who seldom laughed or even smiled, was always strict with his son. He just said "good" when Eric got high grades instead of praising him. On the contrary, Eric had never escaped punishment since he did something wrong. Eric couldn't imagine how his father's students could bear his odd temper. Liam devoted himself to the lab in most of his spare time. What he ordered his son to do was to stick different complex labels to different colorful bottles and jars. And this nearly turned to be the only source of communication between them.

Liam's left arm had a big dark scar, which looked scary and ugly. Thinking his friends may regard his father as a monster, Eric hated the scar and felt ashamed of it.

As Eric was growing up day by day, he started to hate the label-sticking work as well. He'd rather play basketball with his friends than repeat the same boring work. But of course, Liam didn't let him go out and play. Finally, when Liam asked Eric to help him once again, Eric couldn't control his anger and roared to Liam impatiently, "I'm so tired of doing this stupid work! I have my own life and, I don't want to help you anymore!" What beyond Eric's expectation was that Liam didn't say anything, which made Eric a little upset and afraid. After a long silence, Liam sighed and said calmly, "Okay, you're right. After all, you're not a little kid anymore. You are supposed to do whatever you really like."

This entirely surprised Eric. He jumped with wild joy and rushed out of the door. On the way to the park, he looked up to the bright blue sky and large masses of snow-white clouds, kicking the little stones along the road and sang loudly. He was drunk in his own free new world without his father when he suddenly found a strange glass bottle lying on the roadside. Driven by strong curiosity, he picked it up to have a close look. There was a label with *Old Memory* on the bottle. "Wow, I have never seen this kind of medicine." Eric thought, and opened the bottle.

A wonderful scent got into his nose quietly. Eric felt his head aching badly and the pain made him close his eyes. When he opened his eyes, he found himself in the garden outside Liam's lab. Strangely, all the buildings were the old style, just like ten years ago. Eric was surprised and walked nearer.

Unexpectedly, he saw himself. Exactly speaking, it was the five-year-old Eric, who was helping Liam with his work, "Well, I still remained enthusiastic about the work and was willing to help him then." Eric said to himself.

All of a sudden, the sky got dark and the ground started to shake. People on the streets screamed desperately. Countless bricks and glass fell off. "It's the earthquake!" The scene reminded Eric of the disaster ten years ago, which almost destroyed everything, Fortunately, Eric's family survived the earthquake and rebuilt their home.

Eric was recalling the past when a man pushed him rudely. It's Liam! He held the little Eric, covering his little head by his body, and rushed out of the door. "Be careful!" Eric saw a house fell down and trapped Liam immediately. Eric's hand was trembling. He tried to clean the dusty bricks and found the two guys.

The little Eric had already lost consciousness, and Liam was holding two bottles, calling his son difficultly, "Dad, I'm thirsty⋯" After several words, the little Eric closed his eyes again. Liam's face was dirty, mixed with dust and tears. He looked at the two bottles in the hand and then looked at his son. Eric recognized the bottles. One was water and the other was a kind of poisonous liquid, which would burn people's skin. Liam dug in the ruin and only found these. However, the

Do You Hear Me, Little Prince?

label on the two bottles was damaged! Both liquid looked the same in appearance, and they smelled the same as well.

What can I do? Eric was so anxious and afraid. Things were the same with Liam. It was the first time Eric had seen Liam behaved so weakly. He was totally at a loss. Finally, Liam made a decision. Eric couldn't believe his own eyes when he saw Liam poured the liquid in one bottle onto his left arm. Unfortunately, it was not the right one! Liam's skin became burnt and dark rapidly with the serious injury. He used his right hand to open the other bottle and fed the water into little Eric's mouth.

Tears clouded Eric's eyes. He wanted to cry, but couldn't say even a word, as if something blocked his throat. He didn't know the scar on Liam's left arm was because of him. And neither did Liam tell Eric. He regretted what he said and did when a strong smell got into his nose again.

This time when Eric opened his eyes, he was on the bench of the park. He stood up and rushed to the lab as fast as possible. He then understood Liam. Love always has the label such as "smile" "praise" "concern" or "kiss", but these are not the way Liam loved. He was just not so good at expressing his own feelings and didn't find a proper way to tell Eric how much he loved him. His love didn't need any label, and he loved his son deeply with action.

After Eric stuck a new label to a bottle again, Liam patted him on the shoulder, and then both of them smiled.

（作者学校：河北省石家庄市第一中学）
本文为2018年"北大培文杯"决赛参赛文

作者的话

虽然有些老套刻板，但确实，每个深爱着文学的人都离不开写作和阅读，它们是我期盼爬上山巅看日出路上的无言挚友。

一直以来，我看书如痴如迷，并在大量广泛的阅读当中逐渐塑刻出自己心悦的风格，不仅为各种情节的世界背景积攒了多样化知识，也奠定了后来的写作与思想模式。至少目前，反乌托邦风格是我最为喜欢的一种：冷酷的环境引发沉思，客观的旁观者角度总能够让人想起"像一潭死水，激不起一丝微澜"的经典评论。

这篇"欲望之笼"（Cage of Desire），是我对自己喜欢的象征性风格的致敬与表达，通过对秩序与混乱的极端化表现让文章富有戏剧性与矛盾感。文章乍一看并无多大波动，但我想令其产生一种细微而沉重的感染力。一切简单而绝对，但背后还有很多可以通过延伸思考来体现出讽刺性的东西。

更愿自己秉持初心，携一支笔写下明天。

CAGE OF DESIRE

盖雪琪

With excitement and fear that almost overflow with my heart,

Do You Hear Me, Little Prince?

today I'm going to escape from this island— a cage of desire.

Two years ago, some people and I left our homeland by boat to seek a better place to live, for our homeland had become a country full of wars and diseases. People fought for different profits, and wars seemed meaningless and endless.

Catastrophe finally fell on the people on the boat after sailing for more than a half year. We met terrible thunderstorm and gale, which tore apart our boat harshly and made everyone disappear in the big wave without a second to scream.

I woke up on the beach alone, feeling rigid and wet. But I was so weak that I couldn't even move my fingers and open my eyes even little, just with the consciousness of feeling alive. Listening to the smooth wave of the sea for a long time, I finally heard human steps approaching me quickly. I tried extremely hard to open my eyes, but the white stones, the white sand and even the white trees almost made me blind.

I was saved by a man.

After losing awareness of time for a long period, I woke up again on a bed of a hospital. Roughly swallowing the meal near my hand, a woman appeared beside my bed in silence, she made simple self-introduction and introduced this island to me in a still voice. I was observing her as she was making introduction. She wore white uniform and had white hair, what surprised me most was that her irises were even white! Although she smiled friendly, her facial expression really scared me. During her introduction, I got to know that this island was once ruined by war totally years ago. The people survived drew a conclusion that it was the variety of people's life and the richness of colorful material world that made people have endless desire, thus causing crime and war in the end. If people wanted to build a world with peace and without crime, the people here needed to build a world without any color to restrain people into a world without desire.

"What's more," she said, "the crime rate on this island is zero." She lightly smiled again.

This woman would be my daily guide for several weeks. And I decided to go out of the hospital when I felt I was well enough. I stood in front of the mirror to shave my beard and moustache, which made me feel horror of the life here for the first time.

My irises and hair all became white like that woman, and everyone here. And I must wear white clothes like everyone on this island.

"Sorry, but it is the rule here." the woman clarified. They made operations on my body.

The facts proved that my scare to the life here was right.

Everything on this island was white, white clothes, white cars, white house and white skyscrapers. Also, everything here was in strict order, people who broke the order would be seen as criminal, and would be punished by the policeman in a special way— marking different colors on you.

At first, the boring life repeated day by day, which almost made me forget who I was. I still tried to search for different colors by my eyes when I was wandering on the street but always failed at the end. Gradually, I began to walk like a people without soul like everyone on the street.

Do You Hear Me, Little Prince?

This was truly an island without desire.

However, I was punished by the policeman as a terrible criminal, which became a big event on this white island and made all the people not be willing to get close to me, for I kept a green plant privately.

"People can't live without desire, I can't adapt to the life here, I believe." I thought in my mind when I found a seed brought from my homeland occasionally sowed by me in the white soil in my yard began to grow and become a green plant. I decided to keep it privately so that it wouldn't be found by the people here and be changed to a white plant.

However, I was caught by the policemen here and marked a green line on my clothes, which showed clearly everyone that I broke the rules and I was an offender.

I silently saw the scared "white" people when they met me. Instead of shamed, I felt this was an improper world until today.

This was totally a cage of desire.

So, I decided to escape from this island in order to wake up from this horrible "white" dream today.

I ran for a long time until I reached the beach in the darkness brought by the night. And I saw the blue and peace sea with moonlight falling on the surface of the sea like silver for the first time after living in a white world. I felt tears fall from my face constantly.

There was a boat on the beach, which seemed like brought by the god.

After sailing for a while and making sure that island had disappeared under horizon, I stopped at the middle of the sea.

"Endless desire brings catastrophe to people. A world without desire is also a horrible dream to me. Where should I go?"

I hesitated.

(作者学校：山东省东营市一中)

本文为 2017 年 "北大培文杯" 决赛参赛文

GET RID OF THE LABEL "KID"

> ▼ My hopes are not always realized, but I always hope.
>
> ——Ovid

书生意气，挥斥方遒。在本章节中，小作者们摘掉"孩子"的标签，尽情挥洒青春，让年轻的风采一览无余。

这里有校园生活，有与人相处的不知所措，有对亲情友情的深切认知，有在集体生活中的努力适应，也有在人群中成就自我的迫切需要；这里有青春视角下的社会，有青少年眼中人与人、心与心之间的隔阂和伪装；这里有接踵而至的成长烦恼，有面对困难不公时的低落不甘，更有青春的畅想和青春的不羁。

在"媒体变革"的时代背景下，这些青少年作者们拥有更新的视角、更为大胆的创意和不拘一格的思维环境。他们用各种不同形式表现出了青春对于传统的抗争，比如说唱，比如给蜘蛛侠写的信，比如十四岁到四十岁的相互穿越，比如考场上的戏谑杂文……这些巧妙的设计，为文章中的传统主题增添了一份新的色彩。

青春的视角是宽广的，青春的节奏是激昂的，希望每一位成长中的青少年，都能通过自身的努力抗争，完成生命中最美的蝶变。

> **作者的话**
>
> 爱诗歌、爱英文、爱说唱、爱幻想,在这黄金时代里我有很多奢望,想爱,想做梦,想撒丫子跑,想哼出夏夜清凉的旋律,想写下太阳般热烈的诗篇。
>
> 和所有以梦为马的诗人一样,我要做远方忠诚的儿子,做物质的短暂情人,将诗歌的火把高举——此火为大,开花落英于你我火热的胸膛。

METAMORPHOSIS

吴一凡

[Chorus]

You may never been on television or be the one

that your teacher loves to give you *the Student of the Month*.

You may have never been in a champion team

but you might be a star to the world that hasn't been seen.

Hold on and one day you may receive a key in the mail

which helps you unlock the door and wipe off the cloud.

Break the final cocoon and fly out of your prison cell.

The metamorphosis happened and I'm singing it to the whole

world aloud.

[Verse I]

You got a blue collar father and a baby sister to look after.

A common family gave you poverty but nothing other.

You kept waiting for a new chapter,

staring at stars through the gutter.

Your fellows called you weak and liked to beat you down a lot,

when you came alone the block they used to clown a lot.

You tried to see hope,

but always received a bad end;

You tried to rewrite

the script and study was your last chance.

You'd been given nothing but you could take it.

Your were patient in this prison.

You held your dream and you seized it,

believing one day you would make it.

The greats weren't great because they could paint at birth.

The greats were great because they painted a lot.

Night with books and papers, sound of silence got heard.

You kept going, staying awake. You were never enough.

And one morning you received a letter.

——An admission to college. Your hard work paid off altogether.

You'll be traveling across the world and do what you love for work.

After all in Gaokao you've got a seven hundred as a reward.

Get Rid of the Label "Kid"

Take that system, what do you respect.

Generation of kids choosing love over a desk.

Just put those hours in and check for what you get

— a key in the letter that leads you to a brighter next.

[Chorus]*1

[Verse II]

Northwest city, he fell asleep— easy to wake up.

He took a drink and sipped it, hands shaking. He hadn't recovered.

He dreamed back to decades ago when he settled in Xinjiang.

A veteran's life was kind of tough though— whatever game he never won trump.

Time was changing.

Single old man that fell behind couldn't keep up.

No one rang him.

He even got problem getting the cell phone recharged.

He tried to pass his story and glory to the next,

but his old voice and dialect made him hard to connect.

Old friends had got their pot of gold,

or were heading for their heaven road.

Only he was broke,

but he didn't give up hope.

Old names on the diary book.

Kind of love deep in his root.

In the morning he woke up alone,

sweeping the street that he used to own.

He did it for no reason,

like on National Day he put on a suit.

Hearing the National Anthem he stood still and saluted.

A curious kid asked him

why doing so and allowed the old to hug him.

Finally old man got the key in his fate.

When he told the young his story his tears streamed down his face.

[Chorus]*1

[Verse III]

Dirty block, narrow street,

she came home alone.

Seven days she worked in six,

hardly could pay for a room.

Promising future could have been not far away

for the pretty young lady,

but it changed to be crazy after she got a baby.

No way to buy food.

Dropped out of high school.

"He's not a man. He can't provide you."

He didn't want to,

but you kept the baby any how.

Hard way to go through.

"What are you going to do now?"

Get Rid of the Label "Kid"

Her belly was getting bigger.

No one cared the changes in her figure.

Girl of seventeen with a baby, stepfather refused to keep her.

The young couple came up from nothing but for their young faces.

They told her not to get married but she went and did it anyway.

She worked hard. She didn't beg. She didn't borrow.

Night at the factory, day time job at McDonalds.

They finally made it when they didn't know how.

They gained the key on their own to open their new house's door.

[Chorus]*1

[Verse IV]

TV sounded swinging in empty room,

he fell asleep on the coach.

At twelve o' clock he got home.

Lonely city and a house.

His wife waited for him in their hometown.

The reserved man didn't talk much to his son.

Son studied in another city— they must see far.

The family was somehow torn into three parts.

"Temporary goodbye." He was patiently waiting.

From son in kindergarten to college,

it was he who raised it.

Wondering whether it was right or wrong.

Was it worth leaving so long?

When he ran out energy

son's phone call came.

And he got strength from it.

Staring at the railway.

Hearing son's voice he felt safe.

"Son I'm working to change your fate."

As for himself whatever is OK.

The light was still on.

The night was really long.

A sun ray shone on their photo of three, and his life would go on.

On day he got a key in the mail.

Big news: son finally got a decent job.

So the father moved back to his hometown and their old house.

He and his wife even started planning a trip to the south.

[Chorus]*1

[Verse V]

He dreamt of going further but had to stay in the north.

Aiming at a white collar but in a small school he majored in the law.

Dreams were burned to powder.

He just couldn't take it.

Considering learning one more year.

But he knew his strength couldn't make it.

And he got loose.

"There's another way out maybe."

He ever stepped in his school.

Get Rid of the Label "Kid"

Hustling and drinking was his daily.

Ran with a bad bunch.

Climbed up to the roof and had a smoke or two.

Got used to talking through kicks and punch, an outlaw, he broke the rules.

He was battling drag abuse,

getting in trouble with the police.

"What is up with you?"

Used to make the honor roll but now he got no peace.

He planned himself a bright prospect,

a job makes money easy.

But alcohol seemed to build his life unrealistic and dizzy.

I hated him the most, but the story wasn't just over.

One day when his girl asked him about the future

seriously he told her

the tension was heightened so he had to hold the weight on my shoulders.

He would leave her and go to fight as a soldier.

He wasn't bad, he was just an adolescent.

That was easy to blow his composure.

A thug's legendary story had just unfolded there.

In his school work he surely had no good result.

But his final choice sent him a key to stand out.

Now his story I began to love to recall.

To those who really want to change Lord will always give help.

"What's his name?" Well I can't rap it out.

Because he's been a head in army now.

[Chorus]*1

[Outro]

Life can be hard sometimes, and the future may seem like a phantom.

We might become used to being common, afraid to dream.

So our ideal becomes a sanctum.

But everyone can receive their key to their dreams

— everyone is equal.

If you hold on and be strong, trust your ego.

We can let that metamorphosis happen.

Go yelling out your dream and the whole world will echo.

（作者学校：新疆生产建设兵团第二中学）

本文为2016年"北大培文杯"决赛参赛文

> **作者的话**
>
> 我是一个热爱文学的理科生，在我看来，文学是我们的理想国。我们在这里让梦想驰骋，让兴趣生长；我们在这里认识自我并探索生活的可能。在这里，我们可埋下只属于自己的秘密，也可写下想分享给大家的篇章。尽管学理，这个理想国对我而言依旧意义重大。
>
> 理科的严谨并不与文学的浪漫相冲突。我不企望成为如梁思成一般文理兼修的大师，只希望自己能在文学与科学的日月同辉中，领略一个更为精彩的世界。

GET RID OF THE LABEL "KID"

陈渔

Dear Peter Parker, or friendly neighborhood Spiderman,

It's really happy to write to you! As a teenager, I really adore you a lot as you've already become a superhero that fights for the world despite the fact that you are still a teenager. I especially like it when you struggle through failures and eventually get rid of the label "kid" which Ironman attached to you.

The first time you met Ironman was during Civil War when

Ironman broke into your normal life and asked you to do him a favor. Ironman took you by storm at the first glance by his charm that belonged to an experienced mature man only. You made up your mind to be as excellent as him.

However, Ironman always called you "kid", which seemed to be the common shortcoming of all students. He warmed you; he protected you, monitored your deeds from time to time, and praised you just like a parent. If I were you, I would probably be satisfied and have stopped, yet you didn't. You were desperate to grow up to become a warrior to fight with him side by side or even become a knight who owned the capacity to protect him instead of being a little kid who could do nothing but hide behind him.

That was exactly the power which made you different.

You were longing to get rid of the label "kid" and you made it.

You possessed the heart of responsibility that belonged to a mature man. When you accidently got the superpower, you told yourself that you should do something nice with your power and that if something terrible happened because you did nothing, it would be your fault. You suited up and became Spiderman after school to use your power. You would do things as big as chasing evil merchants who sold alien weapons secretly; you would also do things as small as helping the old find their way home. The unknown distance, the uncountable people were all relevant to you. You took on the responsibility to build a better world like an adult would do.

You owned the warmth and kindness that belonged to a mature adult. Since you were not allowed to be the big hero Spiderman, you

Get Rid of the Label "Kid"

chose to be the kind neighborhood Spiderman. You were kind to the cat that lived in the sandwich shop, you smiled at your classmates who envied your good scores and laughed at you. You were even too kind to kill any life including villains, so you chose to stick them with your webs and left them to the police. You had a kind heart that had space for all lives.

You had the ability to reject fake fames. You preferred to attend parties using the identity "ordinary Peter Parker" to show up as Spiderman who would catch everybody's attention. You said "No" when Ironman showed his willingness to introduce you to the world. Whichever degree you were at, you still believed that you were ordinary Peter Parker, and that you were friendly neighborhood Spiderman.

You struggled to gain the bravery and willpower that belonged to a mature adult. You overcame your fear and saved your friends who were stuck in the high-lifter going wrong at hundreds of meters high. Soon later, the great trouble brought out the best part of you. You were buried in ruins by the super villain and no one could come to your aid. You were surrounded by darkness, pain and fear which made you cry desperately like a helpless kid. Minutes later, you decided to overlook any pain and fear and to rescue yourself. You made it through with unbelievable willpower and stood up like a real hero.

With all the qualities, Peter, you finally clawed your way to the top and got rid of the label "kid". One day you told Ironman that you wanted to be as splendid as him, yet he pointed out that actually you were better with great pride. When faced with mighty enemies, Ironman crowned you to announce that you had become a mature Avanger who could fight together with him just like a king would do to his knight.

Eventually you got rid of the label "kid" and grew up. Finally, you became an Avanger who fight for the world he likes and the people he loves.

Dear Spidy, I hope you could have a brighter future as a grown-up, and I could get rid of the label "kid" just like you as soon as possible.

Lots of love!

Your biggest fan

（作者学校：江苏省新海高级中学）

本文为 2018 年"北大培文杯"决赛参赛文

Get Rid of the Label "Kid"

> **作者的话**
>
> 我是一个安静与活泼并存的"并不文艺"少女，平时一大爱好是看新闻，关心时政。不过，我还是坚信，唯音乐与书籍不可辜负，因为当全世界都对你背过身去时，它们不会。读书使人安静，让我们得以与心底的自己重逢。在闲暇时间，我喜欢看电影和追剧，并且达到了痴迷的程度，就像《逃离德黑兰》中说的，"小时候，电影比生活更重要"。初中时，我开始学习声乐和播音主持，喜欢弹吉他。在性格方面，同学们常用"people person"来形容我，大概是因为我性格温和，好相处。
>
> 记得白岩松曾说过，"这世界上总有一些人在以一颗志愿者的心做事情。"我最大的理想是做一名外交官，希望可以通过自己的努力，让世界有一点点改变，让大家更了解我们的祖国。我知道梦想还很遥远，但是，就像我的偶像老白说的那样，"人们声称最美好的岁月，其实都是最痛苦的，只是事后回忆起来的时候，才那么幸福。"我坚信，每个人都可以通过自己的努力，到达心中的远方。最后，以那句英国著名标语作结，希望我可以"keep calm and carry on"。

THE ILLNESS

李淼然

"Elle, can't you just go away? I hate you!" A beautiful girl with curly blonde hair yelled at the pitiful girl standing opposite to her with fury.

Elle smiled. When she was feeling down, she would smile instead of crying.

"Are you smiling? What kind of illness do you have?" The blonde girl shouted again, "I beg you, please, get out of here!"

"How can you treat me like this?" Elle couldn't hold back her tears any longer. As she ran out of the classroom, tears pouring down her cheeks.

It was her freshman year in high school as well as the darkest year in her life. Elle, the ordinary school girl, was ridiculed by others as a heavy girl. It seemed that no one would like her and even her mother gave her a cold shoulder.

Elle did have difficulties getting along with others. She was eager to make friends with her classmates and wanted to be part of them at any cost. She would do whatever they said to please them, but all she received in return was satire and mockery.

What Elle didn't know was when she got out of the classroom, all her classmates clapped for victory, calling the blonde girl "goddess". But now, all she wanted to do was to leave the things behind and have a good cry.

It seemed that God had closed all the doors in front of her without opening a window. Everything in her life was indeed out of control.

She ran to the mailbox, hugging her knees, burying her head in her arms and sobbing violently. Suddenly she found a letter lying on the floor, which had her name written on it. She opened it carefully. Curious and interested, she found a key and a note which said "The key is right in your hand".

Elle stopped crying and wondered, "Who sent it? What's the purpose of giving me a key?"

She cautiously observed the key: a vintage delicate bronze key with a pattern of wings. Then she looked at the note and flashed back to her first day at school. She was shy but got good marks in exams then. Not afraid of being alone, she seldom talked to anyone else.

"Maybe I am ill," Elle thought to herself, "I'm just a girl trying to find a place in this world, but I've cared too much about others' opinions. I've let them drown out my own inner voice. The key is right in my hand." She held the key tightly.

It didn't take much persuasion before she decided to change.

She returned home hopefully, opened her diary and wrote down "I'll start fresh and be someone new".

She put a rope through the key and made it a necklace, carrying it wherever she went.

She worked out regularly, studied harder than ever and learned to express her true feelings. Although her classmates still held the prejudice, they couldn't deny how surprised they felt about her change. No matter what others said about her, she never seemed to care about it.

Day by day, she enjoyed the healthy lifestyle, and eventually became a top student in her class. Her effort was recognized by everyone. She changed herself into a nice and loving girl, and people gradually accepted her.

Her mother took pride in her, calling her "sunshine". The blonde girl made an apology to her and invited her watching movies; people started hanging out with her… Everything has changed, and she no longer felt out of place. Then she was chosen to deliver the commencement speech and was admitted to a top university.

Several years later, she came back to her high school and witnessed a girl weeping in the corner by chance.

Memories flooded back.

Elle came up to the girl, tapping on her shoulder, "Everything will be fine".

The girl choked with sobs, "Why are they being so mean to me? I obey whatever they said to make them happy but they still treated me like this… they always said that I was ill but… am I?"

"No," Elle said, "you've just locked yourself in a dark small room, but the key is right in your hand." She held out her hand and placed the key that she carried for years into the girl's hand. The girl looked at her gratefully in tears.

They both smiled.

（作者学校：河北省邯郸市第一中学）
本文为2016年"北大培文杯"决赛参赛文

> **作者的话**
>
> 我从小喜欢阅读，不过，陈列着众多书籍的书架上最多的还是"哆啦A梦"系列。
>
> 简单来说，兴趣是十分重要的。英语自有美在其中，有时，第一次看见某个单词，就觉得音美；再看，意也美，一瞬间就喜欢上了。这正是语言的魅力。另外，英语作为使用最广泛的语言，也有学习的必要性，出国游学的时候省去麻烦，倒也自在，天下大可去得。

TOM'S ADVENTURE FOR KEYS

周星宇

After looking around, the little boy, Tom, opened the postbox carefully. He was a bit anxious, but of great expectation, due to an appealing story he had heard. If you were confused about your life, you could write a letter and put it into the postbox. Then, you would get the key one day later.

Then, in this red postbox was really a mail. Tom opened it excitedly, but he was deeply disappointed by what he saw. There was no letter he had expected, but a little, yellow item. It was a key, which was giving out a sense of dream. Thinking there must be someone playing jokes on him, Tom turned back, willing to go home. At that time, a door suddenly appeared, colorful and shining. It seemed that someone was calling on him to open the door. Tom couldn't help staring at it, slowly stretching out his arm. The key was closer and closer to the door, and when he finally opened the door, he passed out.

It was a cold night. Tom, aged 40, was walking hard. His coat was too bad to protect himself against the heavily blowing wind. Eventually, he reached his home successfully. He could immediately get into the warm house, enjoying the comfortable sofa and delicious food. However, he hesitated. He was already 40, but his business failed again. He was indeed ashamed to bother his old parents. What's worse, he couldn't bear his brother's sarcasm. After struggling, he finally gave up his desire to warmth and knocked at the door. Out of his expectation, what the house showed him were tolerant smiles instead of faces full of hatred. Delicious food was cooked for him, while his brother encouraged him to try again. After having a sound sleep, the next day, Tom took off again, taking along the courage and warmth he had got from his families.

Slowly, the little boy, Tom, opened his eyes. The sun was shining while birds were singing and he was standing in front of the postbox, aged 14 instead of 40. Nothing was changed but the key, which had turned into a letter. It read, "The family is to someone, what the harbor is to a ship." Getting back home, it was the first time Tom should think his parents were so kind while his playful brother was so lovely.

However, the second day, Tom came back again for he still had

Get Rid of the Label "Kid"

a problem. He believed that he would get the key once again. Sure enough, there was a key as well as a door. With excitement, Tom opened the door.

No wonder that Tom drank so much. He was betrayed by his partner, who had turned all his efforts into nothing. He even thought of death and prepared to make it a reality. Fortunately, someone sat next to him at the same time. It was Jerry, Tom's friend, who hadn't been seen since they arguedten years ago. Then, she crossed thousands of miles for Tom's rescue. "I'll help you. We are friends, aren't we?" When Jerry said with a smile, Tom cried, regretting that he had lost his valuable treasure for a long time, as well as appreciating that it came back to him. Although it was still at night, he saw the sun rising while shining.

Tom wanted to open eyes, but they had been filled with tears, through which he saw the sentence on the letter. "In spite of heavy wind and huge waves, the friendship is an unsinkable ship." With a smile, Tom decided to forgive Jerry for telling his mother the fact that he had not finished his homework.

The next few days, Tom felt happy for he had solved his problems, knowing his family and friends would always be there willing to give him a hand. However, he was sure that something was lost. As a result, again, he stood in front of the postbox, where a mail was waiting. But inside it was no longer a key, but a letter. Filled with excitement and curiosity, Tom began to read it.

"Have you heard of the legendary bird named Shuofang? It is born in the sky, and keeps flying from birth to death, because it has no feet. As a matter of fact, everyone is like a Shuofang. Family gives us a place to take a nap, while friends give us something to depend on. But, after resting, it is you yourself that shake your wings to try to travel afar. You are just the most valuable treasure to you."

Looking up at the sky, it seemed that there was a bird flying. It shook the wings, fought against the heavy wind.

From then on, Tom neither opened the postbox nor sought for the keys. He knew that he had got the keys to life. They were his family, his friends and himself.

（作者学校：重庆市第十八中学）

本文为2016年"北大培文杯"决赛参赛文

> **作者的话**
>
> 我是一个热爱英国文学和电影、具有浪漫主义情怀的理科生。文理之间本无壁，应破之壁在自己。思维与逻辑的碰撞，万事总是相通相似。希望我今后能够坚持本心、矢志不渝，在自己选定的道路上踽踽前行。

THE RULE

王京菁

The tide rises, the tide falls. The leaves rise, the leaves fall. The stones rise, the stones fall. Everything rises, everything falls. My friends, why do you think you can break the rule?

I

After obtaining my doctor's degree I rushed to my high school as quickly as possible. I didn't know if there was anything waiting for me, but a weak voice shouted in my mind all the time: "Go back! Go back⋯" Being pushed by it, I knew it was time to return.

I couldn't continue to escape. I have escaped for nearly ten years after all.

I arrived while students were having class. Looking through a crack, I could see so many innocent and childish faces and most of their owners were rolling their eyes— they were too sleepy.

However, there was something more than just students.

There I saw him again.

To be honest, I didn't recognize him at first sight as it was when I was just 18 years old that I said goodbye to him. Approaching the front door, I could see his face more clearly and hear his voice more truly.

He was my headmaster as well as my physical teacher. I used to call him Mr. Smith.

The first time I saw him, he was just a 28-year-old young man who was tall and straight and always smiled warmly to everyone. Now, however, being in middle age, he was no longer the Mr. Smith I knew.

He had changed a lot, as in my memory he had never had such a fat belly and a hairless head. But in some ways he seemed not to change so much— he still spoke in a loud voice and wore a plaid shirt.

"Who are⋯" he stopped teaching and opened the door, "Johnson? Lily Johnson?"

"Surprised?"

"Shocked, exactly." frowning at me, he continued, "I'm sorry to ask but how⋯"

"Sir, curiosity isn't always a good thing." I interrupted him, "Calm down and talk about something else later. It isn't typical of you to leave students alone, right?" I blinked.

"But⋯" he still stared at me anxiously.

"I said, later. There is no need to be overjoyed although I am also glad to see you again." I forced a smile slowly.

Sunlight shining on his face, just like the first time I saw him. But this time I could see his wrinkle clearly.

II

I guessed no parent would believe that a young and inexperienced teacher could own a superb teaching method. Most importantly, he was just a college student a half year ago.

Also, I guessed no parent would believe that this young and inexperienced teacher's class gained the highest average grade in the first monthly exam.

To tell you the truth, his teaching method was really common but he owned great passion and sense of responsibility that aged teachers had lost. Every word he wrote with chalk was a symbol of his love for his job and his dear students. Every time being reprimanded by him, I could feel his anxiety for us. Every time I listened to him and studied physics, I did feel a sense of joy and satisfaction rising from my mind.

However, the result was still a mess.

"Miss Johnson, I sincerely suggest that you should go over what I taught in class before doing your homework." he handed my exercise book, "Too horrible to look at, ha?"

I stood still in front of his desk. I wanted to tell him how much I love physics and my desperate for it, but what was the use of my struggle? Only outstanding students had rights to confide, hadn't they?

I kept quiet and made a fist secretly trying to stop myself from crying— God knowed how much time I had spent to learn Physics. God knowed how much I liked the man sitting in front of me.

Realizing I didn't want to say anything to argue, he asked me to come and comforted me: "I do understand your feelings and difficulties. I know you are a hard-working and aggressive student who has passion and energy. Perhaps you are not so gifted but it's not so necessary. In my view, you should try to 'understand' the subject."

"Understand?"

"Just feel it."

I showed him a puzzled look.

"Don't see but feel, physics needs to be felt. After feeling it attentively, truth will appear automatically." His eyes were shining.

"Truth, what's it? What's the answer?"

"It is a truth about everything—tide, leaves, stones⋯ everything.

"It is a rule that everything has to obey in the universe." he was so excited that his voice trembled like string.

"That can't be my job, obviously." I sighed deeply.

"If you think you can, you can. Nothing is impossible even if your homework is like disaster." he smiled with encouragement, "It takes time."

His words were so touching that my heart trembled and my soul cracked. After that short conversation, I seemed to be bewitched by him and dived into my fate without any hesitation.

III

I've forgotten, completely. I've forgotten how many times I looked at my terrible report card tearfully. I've forgotten how many times I wanted to give up. I've forgotten how many times I shouted with despair.

I've remembered, clearly. I've remembered every time he smiled at me. I've remembered every time he caressed my head and said "you can". I've remembered how many exercise books I've finished. I've remembered the feeling of taking the first place.

At that time, I thought I've won.

Holding my report card, I went to his office. I didn't know if there was anything waiting for me but there was a voice asking me to do so. Being pushed by the voice, I knocked at his door.

"Come in." he glanced at me and continued to work, "Something matters?"

"Yes, sir, very important." I approached him carefully, "I am here to…"

"You did really a good job." he stopped working and stared at me, "What praise do you want? Another pile of text papers? I suppose you won't be interested in chocolate."

"That is not… not the point." I said excitedly, "I want yo…"

"I guess book is still the best choice." he interrupted and gave me a book.

"*Letter from an Unknown Woman.*"

"Zwick's. An excellent book." he smiled warmly, "It will be

beneficial for you, I think."

Was I refused? I didn't know exactly.

I left his office clumsily. Standing by the door, I asked: "Mr. Smith, may you hug me? As another praise."

He shook his head mildly: "Don't be like the unknown woman. Without me, you can make more achievements."

At that time I was 17 and he was 28.

IV

After the college entrance examination, I went to the university he was graduated from. I majored in physics.

I bought me a plaid shirt the same as his.

As time went by, I realized every word he said was true—without him, I did achieve more. After hard work, I gained a chance to the University of Cambridge for a doctor's degree, and I rushed to England without hesitation.

I used to invite him to travel in England but he refused as he was too busy.

Time and tide wait for no man. I couldn't believe the last time I saw him was ten years ago.

"If you are tired⋯" he passed me a cup of tea, "Go back home."

"Returning to the origin is not a good idea." I supped the tea, "And these days I think I am approaching one thing."

"What?"

"The rule!" I shouted excitedly, "I can sense it."

"Stop, Lily, stop." his expression was difficult to read, "You are a girl, my gosh, a girl. physics is always man's game, you know, you are not really talented···"

"You've changed sir, a lot." I said incredibly, "You've said I can run after the rule!"

"Run?" he pointed at my artificial limbs, "Even though you are disabled?"

I was speechless and didn't know how to argue. Turning my wheelchair, I didn't want to face him— he seemed to be right after all.

"You don't need to feel sorry. You should be happy that I haven't lost my hair like Plonk." I turned around and tried to force a smile but failed.

V

A car accident had broken my peaceful life. I lost my legs when I was just 19. It sounded like an outdated story, right? But I was sorry to tell you it was true.

When I was taken to hospital, I could hear screaming and smell odor of AQ Steril. It seemed that my soul was going to leave my body and won't come back again.

When I was awake, I soon realized that my legs had been amputated. I tried to reach them but there was nothing but sheets. Feeling hopeless, I wanted to end my useless life but there was always a voice shouting in my mind: "The rule··· the rule··· you are near!" Being pushed by it, I went back from windowsill.

Sitting in my wheelchair, I went back to the university and finally I gained the chance to Cambridge.

VI

Being pushed by him, I "wandered" with him on the campus.

"Sir, I think I'm getting to understand Physics." I asked him to stop, "You know, the rule for everything. When I was little I really hated my fat and ugly legs and now I lost both of them. When I fell in love with you, I thought I would die without you. When I was in Cambridge I made a boyfriend, but now he is no longer important. Nothing is necessary, even including me. Everything has their glorious period. Everything will be at the bottom in their life time. Nothing can escape the rule, nothing can escape their contabescence. The tide rises, the tide falls. The leaves rise, the leaves fall. The stones rise, the stones fall. Everything rises, everything falls. During life, and everyone think they will win but no one of them have made it."

"You," I pointed at him, "and I both will be losers."

He stared at me incredibly.

"Sir, as praise, may you hug me?"

He bent down and hugged me deeply. It seemed that he wanted to warm my soul.

Finally, I drew my hands back and pushed him away.

（作者学校：山东省东营市胜利第一中学）
本文为2018年"北大培文杯"决赛参赛文

> **作者的话**
>
> 像所有爱做白日梦的梦想家一样，我擅长神游。凝视天空十五秒，我已在云端遨游一圈。因为眼底的远方，文学成了我背后的翅膀，我飞过乞力马扎罗的雪，寻找豹子的足印。像所有孜孜不倦的猜谜者一样，我热爱生活的谜题，解谜就像同住在镜子里的人对话，近在咫尺的谜底总隔着一层薄壁。因为心头的好奇，文学成为脑海中翻译的梦语，我泛舟赤壁之下，聆听苏子的人生智慧。像所有怀揣理想的游子一样，我寻觅精神的故园，因为脚下的征途，文学成了家园。走进文学的世界，就像回家，在那里，时间可以凝固，瞬间即是永恒。回家，褪去焦灼，汲取力量，更有面对生活的勇气与底气。回家，为了那份"心有所归的无量幸福"。

IT HAPPENS

车子涵

The tide rises, the tide falls.

I can't believe I've been sitting here all day just watching the sea tides. Here, on the berm, above the shore, a place belonged to the lonely. For me, it's like an escape from the madding crowd. A getaway.

Here, I heal myself and rebirth, hold on to the good things in life.

I don't want to lie: I really miss the good old days when I had everything: youth, beauty, fortune, name. My father was a businessman, he was harsh when it came to his business, but very kind to his family, especially me. He taught me a lot of cool stuff, including which most people found inappropriate for a girl in those days. I grew up to be a well-educated lady with a strong mind. It was years after that I finally realized my father wanted me to be tough for a reason.

Sometimes, when things go smoothly for a long time, you naturally expect it to last forever. But that's never the case. When I was eighteen, life almost completely fell apart. First a serious disease swept through my hometown, took away my mother and brother. Then my father's business went down. It was said that he was involved in some kind of an international business crime, but I couldn't imagine a good and loving man like my father should lie to have more money. It almost got me down for a whole year, but I managed to be back on my feet. I was on my own. I left my hometown and tried to make a living in this crazy world.

I was broke. I started with small things, table-waiting and babysitting and cleaning. Young and naive as I was, I knew this wouldn't be always. I just knew I would do something greater. When I got tired at the end of the day, I just closed my eyes and tried to picture my hometown, that small city near the sea. I remembered every bay, every shore, and every berm. As I pictured the scene, seeing that magnificent view of the sea with scarcely stripes of foams stroking the bay like giant dolphins breaking the surf, I was content. I could see the

Get Rid of the Label "Kid"

tides rise and fall in my head, and I told myself, the tide rises, the tide falls. Life is up and down. Everything will be okay in the end. If it's not okay, it's simply not the end.

You don't want to hear how I got through those hard days, all those struggles and tears and pain. And how I met someone who offered me a shoulder to cry on when I finally took off the mask of toughness once in a while, how I found people who got my back, there's no need to bore you with details. Let's just say that I realized I wasn't alone. But I never really walked out of the shadow completely. Inside the chamber of my heart lied a bleeding string that was never really cured.

As I stumbled on my way to a better future, I wasn't lucky all the time. In fact, I was unlucky most times. So when things were finally going my way, I was more amazed than relieved. Though I always knew this would happen at some point, I was still more grateful than ever. I created a new life based on the ruins of an old one. I made it.

Now you may think this is a story of a princess who got over the difficulties and lived happily ever after. Very cheesy, very old school. But the story didn't end. Turned out I wasn't a princess therefore couldn't have the luck to be happy forever. I made it for once, but it didn't last. I don't want to talk about the man who promised to love every wound of my heart but instead left me one more wound to heal over time.

I'm a middle-aged woman now. I have a kid who just left for college. I moved out of the big city and went back to my hometown. My friends wanted me to stay, but I'd made up my mind. I just had to come back to the berm, even just to sit and watch the bay, the shore, the sea. These are the things I've been familiar with since childhood, yet it still blows my mind every time. I need the serenity so bad. The soft wave of the sea is like a gentle hand, it caresses my wounded heart. The rolling tide rises and falls, it's a perpetual circuit, like a promise that life will go on, no matter how bad our losses are. That it will be good again. Even after all, I still believe it will come back around. I just do, deep in my heart, though I still worry.

The twilight of my life is nowhere far. I can't say I still believe in love the way as youngsters do, and I don't know if I trust destiny. Well, actually I never trust destiny. I guess I trust nature. The law of nature is like the tide that comes and goes. I believe I wouldn't be down forever. It is true. But will I ever find the sweetness again— The sweetness of the happy life I once had? Maybe I can leave out the cliché everyone persuades, don't rely on anybody, living on my own. Or I can just hang on, sling the past over my shoulder, move on and never stop.

It's a breathtaking view, the sunset here. Orange and purple clouds are burning the horizon, even setting the water on fire, making it a flaming golden ocean. Suddenly I have an odd feeling of déjà vu, as I watch the tide, the little girl I was decades ago came to me again. I wonder what happened to her, I miss her. She was so tough, so determined, never giving up. I can't let her down. I would never let her down.

Suddenly I want to smile, at all the things I've been through, at all the things that will come. How can I avoid the world to be alone? That's weak. I will be who I am.

Get Rid of the Label "Kid"

My fate is up to me, and I will make things better.

The tide rises, the tide falls. Having been sitting here all day, I feel a little light-headed, but my soul is filled with energy, as if I'm back in those days, being nothing but fearless and young.

Good things will happen to me. If it's a little late, I'll just call it a surprise. After all, it happens.

（作者学校：浙江省宁波市效实中学）

本文为2018年"北大培文杯"决赛参赛文

> **｜作者的话｜**
>
> 素歆五羖才略，思慕四皓高风，梦窥三坟二典，一朝披锦培文。
>
> 似使十载泪蜡，铺筑九霄云程，帆进八纮七地，六翻惊风奔浑。

VICISSITUDES

黄航

The tide rises, the tide falls. Against the azure expanse of sky, the blue sea beckons. Crisp minds caress the tides amorously and groan many compelling stories about the sea and the sailors.

Ted, whose name was homophonic with "tide" in the local accent, was the son of sailors and reared on tales of the sea, thus having a deep affinity to this glamorous and uncharted world. A common phenomenon among the local sailors was that the sense of independence was bred into children at an early age. Granted that the life on the sea was full of uncertainty which resembled the uncontrolled ebb and flow of tides, those who were destined to be sailors had to learn how to feed their own mouths and get accustomed to the enigmatic changes of life. So

Get Rid of the Label "Kid"

was Ted.

By some freak of fate, Ted had an instinct of sailing, and the skills in catching fish, which left nothing to be desired. Beyond anyone's anticipation, Ted took an excursion to a remote island for leisure and brought back ten sharks he killed, establishing his renown as the first sailor to wrestle with sharks. The tide rose, and so did his life. The peerless capacity bred the fragrance of fame and fortune, and kindled his yearning for farther adventures. The tide rose.

Youngsters usually entertained a relentless ambition, which gave people enormous vitality and stubbornness. Ted prepared a large boat and embarked on a distant navigation toward the unmapped area that practically no one had entered before. A couple of days on the sea later, Ted spotted an unnamed island covered with lush vegetation. He accounted it a perfect place for hunting and burst into rapture.

Obviously, another handsome harvest was near at hand but all of a sudden, a blast stormed to the boat and chilled the sailors to the bones. A tornado reared its ugly head and carried them to that island gruffly. A misfortune often entailed another. The island mentioned was imagined to be a sanctuary of preys but factually turned the sailors into preys. Nefarious snakes abounded and contributed to a brutal disaster, reducing the crew to solitary Ted, who eventually gave way to the fate and returned home with the dilapidated boat.

The tide fell, and so did his life. The death of other sailors laid a burdensome mortgage on Ted's feeble shoulder and taught him a lumber some lesson of the ups and downs of life. Ted reduced to a church mouse and squandered time in a filthy casino. A man who won in shark fight, and lost in a plight. He became a rootless kite added to those gamblers. The tide fell.

The God of Destiny knocked on Ted's door the second time. A handsome sum of money passed into his pocket by some good luck, or arguably, the casino made it possible to reawaken Ted's life. The longing to the bottomless abyss of ocean beckoned him and rekindled the determination to sail again.

Ted bought a more secure ship with lessons learned and buckled up for another long journey. The wax and wane of fortune was beyond anyone's capacity but attracted people all along. In Ted's nature there was unyielding quest for excellence and uncompromising vigor. His second navigation could bail him out of the dismay inflicted on him by the first one, and would also end as a flap likewise, instead. It was hard to predict or foresee and could only be left to the discretion of the vicissitudes of life. But at least, the tide rose again.

Legend had it that in the deep sea lived a colossal monster that sometimes tore sailors into pieces. At the mere mention of the stories about it, Ted had a sense of impending doom but didn't stop his sailing, in which one couldn't anticipate what would happen next but could grapple whatever he met with, with the finite capacity and the infinite valor.

Coincidentally the monster made an appearance. The skyline got somber from all directions of the compass. The placid water began to howl like a beast. The ship was subsiding into a scary whirl, and the sailors separated from each other in the ensuing panic, with most of them passing out due to the fear.

Get Rid of the Label "Kid"

When Ted came to himself and found that the surroundings were safe, he felt extremely lucky to be alive. But the monster which had caused several deaths already appeared again, and moved to Ted. He had no choice but to combat the devastating creature with his weak harpoon. The imminence of death promoted him to fight resiliently and valorously, with great perseverance and grit that were bestowed to humankind only. He declared war on the vicissitudes of life. At any cost, he defended to death the only hope for life.

At last silence reigned with the departure of the monster. But the silence was then pierced by the roaring sounds of tides. The tide rose and so did Ted's life. The tide fell and so did Ted's life. The tide rose and fall, day in, day out, and so did Ted's life. Ted's life was filled with ebb and flow and fight always.

To quote J. K. Rolling, "Life is difficult, and complicated, and beyond anyone's total control and the humility to know that will enable you to survive its vicissitudes." Life is both rosy and elusive, the uncertainty of which is hard to grasp. It is unsettled, uneven and unknown, like the tide. Humankind is blessed with the courage to battle with it. With the lapse of time, the tide rises and falls and brings the color of life. A man is not only weathered but also strengthened by the vicissitudes of life.

（作者学校：四川省绵阳南山中学）
本文为 2018 年"北大培文杯"决赛参赛文

> **作者的话**
>
> 我热爱阅读，高中三年通读了王小波、鲁迅、王尔德、柏杨和米兰·昆德拉等作家的作品，其中最喜爱的作家便是王小波，他书中的"以人为本"和"三大反对"等思想对我的写作、生活和思考产生了重大影响。也是通过王小波，我学会了批判地看待问题，对一切保持谨慎态度。读着读着，也会想自己写些东西，而我大多只是在生活有感悟时记录下自己点滴的思考，日后回看时，这些思考或许会成为我灵感的来源。本人虽然不才，但也在《长沙晚报》和《湖南教育》杂志上有拙作发表。

BACK

杨寒琦

"How I wish I could live again!" At the last moment of my life, I thought to myself.

……

"Get up! Get up!" A voice suddenly appeared. "This time, you can live again. You can make up for your past mistakes or enjoy your new life. But you only have ten days."

"Who are you?" I asked, but no one answered me.

Get Rid of the Label "Kid"

When I opened my eyes, I was lying on the hospital bed with a lot of medical devices on my body. "I'm alive!" I cried out happily. But I couldn't make any noise because I was too weak to speak.

"I am sorry to inform you, that there are only a few days left for your father." A doctor said to my daughter who was in despair.

"No! I am alive, I won't die!" I wanted to yell at them, but, in fact, I just screamed in my head.

"Why, Dad? Why is God so cold? Why does he want you to die so young? You're only 65! I told you not to drink so much, but it is too late for you now." My daughter, Lisa, said sadly.

"Right! If I had listened to my daughter, I would not have died so young, leaving my wife and daughter suffering." Thinking of this, a drop of tear crossed my cheek and dripped on the pillow.

Tired as I was, I fell asleep with my regrets for my family. It was the tenth before the last day.

……

"No!" I screamed, waking up from my bed and gasping heavily.

"What's wrong?" A woman's voice came up, "Did you have a nightmare?"

Suddenly, I realized that this voice was my wife's voice. Looking at the mirror, finding that I was back to my forties.

"What a shock! Without death, I became younger." I said.

"Don't be silly! We still have to go to work tomorrow, don't say anything stupid and go to bed!" My wife fell asleep after saying this.

Having trouble falling asleep, I thought to myself that I must change my life. Considering I had memories of my life, I could do better than anyone else. I could get a promotion, a better job, a big house and a better education for my daughter.

However, everything would not go as smoothly as I expected. Even if I had memories of my life, there would still be something to disturb you.

Why was it so difficult to change my life?

At night, tired as I was, I fell asleep. It was the ninth before the last day.

……

Then, I was back to my 18-year-old. And, I only got one day left. Although I wanted to change my life and make up for the previous mistakes, it was too hard. I screwed up everything. I didn't get a promotion, and I didn't get a better life. Even worse, I didn't quit drinking, still being addicted to alcohol. It turned out that I couldn't change my life even though I knew everything in advance. Now, I wanted to be a good child, but I just couldn't control my temper, always fighting with my parents and friends. "Old habits die hard", maybe, it was impossible to change one's life.

Tired as I was, I fell asleep. There was no day before the last day.

On the last day, I became a baby. Although I spared every effort to change my fate, it was useless. Through these experiences, I understood that we only had one life, so we must firmly grasp it and make full use of it so that we could live the life we wanted. But it was too late for me to realize that.

Now, I can hear the god of destiny setting the clock of my life. My life is in the bottom, but you haven't. Please make the most of your life, and don't let yourself regret it after dying.

Ten

Nine

Eight

……

Two

One

Zero!

（作者学校：湖南省长沙市周南中学）

本文为2017年"北大培文杯"决赛参赛文

> **作者的话**
>
> 我穿梭于这个平行的世界，在每个时空扮演着不同的角色。
>
> 我在图书馆静静阅读，让情感与灵感在笔尖下流淌；我在体操馆演绎舞蹈，让汗水和笑容渲染青春的画卷；我在音乐厅尽情演奏，在提琴的悠扬旋律中体悟世界；我在实验室默默坚守，用热爱与坚持推开科学的大门。
>
> 当平行宇宙重叠后，便有了你所看到的——完整的我、多元的我。
>
> 在我眼中，写作是心灵的表达，汉语和英语在思维方式和表达上都有其独特的魅力。

THE LOCKED DOORS

刘沛松

"Our fear didn't come from the locked door, but the isolation between our hearts…"

When I was 8, I always climbed on a giant tree and looked up to the starry sky. Once as I listened to the birds, a tick voice hit me. Without any consideration, I rushed to the mailbox and opened it. There

Get Rid of the Label "Kid"

laid a key, one with exquisite pattern and golden light shining on it.

I frowned. It was weird that I received a mysterious key that I didn't know what it was used for. I grabbed it and went to my room. I inserted it in my door and hold my breath. With a pleasing voice, the door opened. I widened my eyes and opened my mouth. An idea struck in my head so I rushed to the other doors. Out of my expectation, it all worked! I tried my best to keep myself from screaming out loud. The magical key shone the light of hope and amazement. I fancied the things behind the doors.

On the next morning, the rain blurred everything outside the window into green and gray smudges. The clouds were dense and opaque which made me kind of frustrated. I put my secret key in my pocket and set out.

I stood at the street, staring at these locked doors. It was confusing that those people isolated them from the others by doors. "What are they fearing of ?" I mumbled.

I walked straightly to the 122B, my friend Susie lived there. To be honest, she was the first person that came in my head as I realized the magic of the key. She was positive and smiled all the way in my eyes. Alex, his father remained good impression for me. Although I only met him for several times, I was sure of his kindness from his smile.

I unlocked the door as I thought. A fierce sound of crashing made me alert. Then it came out a voice of a man. It was furious, filled with dirty words. Then I heard the faint voice of a girl. I moved forward cautiously, and then I watched a dread scene that I wouldn't forget forever. Alex was in a red face, holding a bottle of alcohol. Susie was kneeling on the floor, bleeding, weeping. I heard the heartbroken voice and ran away. I cried all the way, replaying the scene in my head. I was kind of regretting to open the door. But it happened, and it was the truth. I looked at the key, its color faded, possibly because of the agony and fear.

I wandered in the street, looking for the next place. The street turned to a red slop, grass growing on the sidewalks, and the store sagged in the squares. The store played an important role in my childhood. Susie and I bought candy, cookies secretly and enjoyed the sweetness of freedom. I walked close and found some money on the porch. "This must belong to Ms. Smith." I mumbled. I unlocked the store and stepped in.

The store was filled with a smell of cigarette which made me cough. "Who's there!" a furious voice struck me back.

"Me, Jane Lee."

"What the hell are you doing there? Got you, little thief!"

"No! I am not. I just have a magical key, it can unlock all the doors."

He burst into sarcastic laughter.

"Trying to cheat me with those treat in fairy tales? Well, my fists will end the farce!" He lifted his fists.

"Wait, I'm here to ask, is that yours?" I trembled, showed him the money. The anger in his eyes disappeared, in a flash.

"Of course, that's mine⋯" he took the money and went away. He gave me a sharp look as he stopped at the corner.

I was dizzy.

I asked WHY in my head over and over again.

Get Rid of the Label "Kid"

WHY the things behind the door were so different?

WHY people all locked their doors?

WHY there were so many agonies and gloominess behind the door?

The color of the key darkened to black. Then I tossed the key away pettishly, and stood cogitating.

The rain stopped. A beautiful sound of piano lit my heart and I followed the music to a house.

The door of the house opened widely, beautiful music went to every corner of the street through the door. I hesitated. Although the door was opened, I still felt scared for some unknown reason.

"Come in, my dear guest!" It was a voice of a man.

I stepped cautiously into the room. As the man appeared in my eyes, his face blurred as my tears rolled down.

I had heard of his stories. He was the "crazy man" in people's words. It was said that he always opened the door, but her never stepped out. But I felt warm and moved at that time.

"Why didn't you lock the door?" I asked.

"You mean the door? Ah, it's useless."

I looked at him in confusion.

"Just as you did, you opened your heart and came in my place. And those who didn't open their heart will never knock on the door. As for me, there are doors after doors outside the house, not in the rooms, but in our hearts. Since they all locked their door, there's no need to lock mine."

I enjoyed the music, fighting tears in my eyes. I could feel his heart and I knew that this was the real door that the key unlocked.

These memories had vanished for years as mist with sunrise.

Every time I told my friends about it, they laughed in disbelieving.

And I smiled.

I'm waiting for the one who unlock his door of heart for me.

（作者学校：北京市十一学校）

本文为2016年"北大培文杯"决赛参赛文

> **作者的话**
>
> 喜欢语言与文学，心里总藏着去探险或是考古的奇怪愿望，这份愿望可以寄托在文字和书本里。总之，探索这件事，不论是在字里行间还是在过去或未来，仿佛都可以一直做下去。"无尽的远方，无数的人们，都与我有关。"

CHASE WITH THE TIDE

王鼎

The tide rises, the tide falls. It appeared to be a rule for Chase. The ocean remained the color of dusk, which mixed pink, purple and glittering gold. At first the view was lovely, Chase thought, but now it was dull.

He came from an arid desert. Sunset chaser was his long-dead family career. "He was born to chase, to seek." This saying was from his mother who explained his name.

Chase started his journey on his birthday night, when people from his family had considered him to be a grown-up. He had passed deserts, cities, dozens of forests, scores of orchards. Now, with the rising tides, here he was. The destination of his chasing was in front. Once he successfully passed this area, he would succeed.

He found a camp by the sea. It held incenses, with a warm and cozy atmosphere. "Come," a red-haired short lady called him, "have a rest."

Chase studied her face. The woman owned auburn tresses and fair skin, but most importantly, her smile was an honest one. He could tell these after such a long journey. So, he went inside.

The air hung a smell of cinnamon and parsley. Chase entered the camp, feeling the sense of arriving home. Staring at him, the strangers, which were just a small group of three, stopped their chatting. They kept silence just like Chase's desert.

Among them, an aged man broke the ice. "Welcome, my friend," he curled his lips, "may I share the honor of knowing who you are and where you go?"

"You are rude enough", said another elder. His sharp blue eyes glimpsed. "Why not invite him to sit? Our little dove must want a young man to spare an effort on the seduction of old bones!" He laughed.

It was then Chase noticed a maiden, hiding her face in the shadow of the veil. She began to speak with a gentle tone, "Great to meet you, sir."

Chase sat down with a jumping heart. He wondered where he has entered. These three were strangers just met— just like him to them. Yet they showed a tranquil understanding, "Pleased to join you, sirs, and m'lady."

"I, as you can see, am a sunset chaser. This was a family-run business very long time ago. We captured the beam of falling sun to live. Nowadays sunsets are difficult to find, so I have sought for a long time".

"Your dream reminds me of mine," said the second aged man who was called Flip. "I used to want to be a time traveler. In the chaos and turbulences, I tried, very hard. Then I quitted. The road you've taken is full of terrors, I believe. Quit, young man, before you drown in sorrow."

"Alas, the tide rises, the tide falls." The first elder sighed, "I suggest we make our road tomorrow morning as now is getting dark. With this gallant youngster, we shall face no danger. Why not go to bed now? Rosamunde will lead us."

The short woman appeared in silence. She lit four candles to guide them. Chase yawned. Thinking that he will catch sunlight very soon, he slept for the second time on his journey with a cautious but joyful heart.

The very next day they set off. On the breakfast table, Chase drank to wash down bacon and the tales of Old Flip. His determination wandered with the advice Flip gave him. Quit, he said yesterday. The very danger always hid in the tide, in the last trip of the whole venture. He mused, when they slowly travelled afoot. Flip kept saying the house in his childhood, the lemon orchard that buried his parents, his beloved, his first kiss and the last wave-by. "You'll regret that you leave here, your home. Don't you have treasure you hold dear?"

Chase glanced back. The elder and the maiden were just behind. He remained silence. His heart fled back to his puppy love. "I swore to marry her, my Yvonne." Chase thought with a bitter heart. "How many years have passed by? What, five years, seven years? She must have married to someone else. She won't wait me." Chase sighed in his heart.

"Why you chose to pick up your family's career?" the elder behind them suddenly asked, after a long silence, "A sunset chaser is rare to find."

"Yes." Chase answered. He listened the tides as if they would bring him answers. "My mother wanted… that." He remembered the warmth of her palms, her gentle tone, her busy steps, and her will. He watched the waves. The ocean wasn't choppy but rather quiet. He watched the foghorn and the lighthouse. Nothing but emptiness grabbed his heart. He could have married Yvonne, and he could have held his mom's palm when she closed her eyes forever. Now he miserably chased something he might never get.

"I want to see the sunsets. It must be lovely," the girl coughed, "but you see I am seriously ill. I can't handle the illness that stole my sap." She closed her eyes as if the sun's glittering beam would burn her ill and weak eyes.

Chase said nothing. He shouldn't enter that camp. Now he only wanted to get back. They were more dangerous than the monsters he had faced. No doubt, the splashing echoes of the waves enlarged his worry and fear. But this morning he took sacred vows to protect them, and the chivalry grown in him wouldn't allow him to leave them.

"Your answer," the elder shook his head, "didn't come from a man with determination, with success. Other's wishes shan't hinder your own will. Listen this, or you shall be another falling tide just like our Flip."

Get Rid of the Label "Kid"

"I want to be a time traveler." Flip argued, "He and me have different problems." Flip bridled his donkey. "Now, I will stop. There is an inn nearby, in the forest. I will leave you companion."

"Mr Flip!" cried the maiden, "it's dangerous!" but Flip did not listen. His donkey slowly carried him to that forest.

He was no knight, Chase thought, "You shouldn't call him 'sir', my lady." He said, and the girl answered him with tears.

That evening, this group of three slept on the beach, under the rock. Chase couldn't sleep with satisfaction. It was a raining and wet night, which reminded him of the swamp he passed. He almost lost himself in that treacherous swamp. A middle-aged woodcutter saved him. "Hold your dream," he encouraged Chase, "you must enjoy it. Don't take my road with no dream."

The next morning was still raining. Chase settled the elder with warm fire and carried the maiden into the forest. She claimed there was a hospital she travelled so long to find. "Maybe after treatments I can see the sunset. I can't wait. My illness sucked my soul."

The rain was pouring. The girl silently slept on his back. Their clothes were wet. When they reached a river, Chase turned his head, only to find the maiden had passed away in sweet sleep. Her lips curled with joy and hope. Her pale cheek became even a little bit rosy when the rain stopped and the sun appeared. Chase used his sword to dig a grave in this forest. A feeling of warm liquid filled his eyes when he put her into the grave. "I want to see the sunset." She once said. The hope of the splendid sunset and finding a doctor drove her here. But during this very last journey, the passion turned to fear and death.

"Farewell, dreamer," Chase waved to her body, "I will see the sunset."

Chase returned, to find the elder still waiting. "You could go. Where do you want to go?"

"Where is the girl?" the elder asked. His expression told Chase he had already known, and he just needed a final prove, a final announcement.

"She's gone," Chase said, "in her sleep. I suppose there is no pain."

"Good." The elder sadly smiled, "She is a good girl. She is braver than Flip, even than us."

"Yes!" Chase finally ended the conversation, "Let's go!"

"Now," the elder asked when they started to leave, "What's your answer then?"

"Seeking is the only truth," Chase repeated, "the most monstrous devil lives in my heart."

It was then getting dark. The sun was going to set. They ran out of the dim forest.

"You know the tides?" the elder pointed the sea, "what is dead may never die, an author once wrote. The tides prove me this. Now you've fulfilled the dreams of Flip and the little dove girl."

Both of them peered at the world's end. Across the sea, there were no lands, no oceans, no creatures. Nor did it have beauty and curio. Once only the sun could reach here, but now they were here too.

They watched the sun getting down. The tide was rising, harder and stronger than anytime, anywhere. The dancing wave raged against the burning sky.

"I can't count how many times I've been here," the elder suddenly said, "it's time for me to leave."

"What? Wait, who are you? Where will you go?" Chase cried after the back of the elder.

"I come from a different diversion." The old man said, "And I shall go to another."

"You are a time traveler?"

"Well, I am you— a failing version." He disappeared in a flicker. His voice echoed with the choppy and mysterious ocean, with the setting sun and glamorous splendor. The tide fell.

（作者学校：广东省广州市执信中学）

本文为 2018 年"北大培文杯"决赛参赛文

> **作者的话**
>
> 从诗意的寒冬到火热的盛夏,"北大培文杯"陪我走过了充满惊喜和收获的一年。初赛的 The Generation of Pop 让我和"北大培文杯"结缘,开始了我的英语作文梦幻之旅。复赛的科幻作文 Good Helpers,让英语和科幻碰撞出畅想未来的火花。在北京大学的校园中,决赛瞬间的灵感成就了一个 New Me。感谢"北大培文杯"和所有辛苦付出的老师们,让语言文字的繁花在每一个学子的心中绽放。

NEW ME

卓思岑

To tell you the truth, when I saw this topic, I was frozen.

Maybe I was too nervous, or I couldn't wake up from my sweet Peking Roast Duck dream. Anyway, I forgot the meaning of the word "Label". I felt like falling into a deep and freezing hole. I even couldn't breathe the cold air in the splendid room. It was a nightmare for me. How could I? How could I forget such an easy word in this kind of important situation? If I were that girl waiting in Peking Hotel one hour before, I would open my English dictionary to check or memorize more basic words. If I were lucky enough, maybe I could review this word accurately.

Well, it was a truth that I had already forgotten this word. The only thing I could do was to do something to recall my poor memories in the pandemonium. I looked around the room: all the students were in green, like avocados and kiwi fruits. It seemed that they all knew the meaning and their pens were flying like unidentified flying objects on the sky of paper. What's more, I even saw someone smile! That was incredible! That made me feel even worse. I was so ashamed that I wanted to flee from the crowd, even by crawling.

Actually, I'm one of the top students in my hometown. In my teachers' point of view, I'm an excellent girl. So, they call me "Talent Girl". In my friends' point, they admire me for the fluency of English and Korean. Sometimes, they come to me and ask me the secret of learning. They call me "Top Girl". And my parents always force me to do many exercises. However, I don't like it at all. But I must try my best to achieve their expectations. Otherwise, I'm just a joke.

But now, I'm nobody. Maybe when l come back to school next month, all the teachers will criticize me. Maybe my classmates will laugh at me. Maybe my parents will be disappointed with me. I almost cry out! I just want to tell them: I'm not a perfect girl. Your expectation makes me stressed out! In my childhood, I have got no time to play games or communicate with friends. Even I couldn't read the *Little Prince*'s fantastic and dramatic story! The growth of the rose in 221BC never stopped to wait for an innocent but tired girl. When I saw it finally, it was already ripe. I missed the best part. I want to be the girl I wanna be! So please don't put labels like "Excellent" or "Talent" on my body! I'm a rebellious and creative girl! I want to throw all the labels in the rubbish bin!

Oh, wait… wait… Oh my god! The feeling was like seeing the light from the darkness. It was the very first breath when my head had been drowning under the water. I know the meaning now! My heart almost jumped out of my throat! After a while, something grew from the depth of my heart. Just as the old saying says: "You're not somebody, you're nobody." They always stick labels like "Excellent" on my body, which makes me anxious. I can't put myself in an absolutely correct position with them. Now I want to get rid of the labels. I am just a common girl, a senior high school student. And the only thing I'm doing is to attend the competition. It's holding on though the road is long. The results are not essential now. I just gonna be free and enjoy the journey of writing.

OK, I'll start writing now! Please look at the new me!

（作者学校：四川省成都市树德外国语学校）
本文为 2018 年"北大培文杯"决赛参赛文

> **作者的话**
>
> 朱光潜说过:"凡是文艺,都是根据现实世界而铸成另一超现实的意象世界,所以它一方面是现实人生的返照,一方面也是现实人生的超脱。"语言是用于表达的工具,文学是展现心灵的艺术。我写的故事超脱现实,于是,我能在这个虚构的世界里看到比现实更加鲜明的人物性格与略带夸张的心理历程,而每一个虚构角色都是一个极端化的现实人物的映射。文学创作,或许就是由此反观现实,达到"旁观者清"。

UNDER MY SKIN

陈佳怡

I

At eight o'clock, an hour after his alarm clock went off, Thomas woke up sweating from a nightmare. Surviving from his intense bad dream, he took a long breath before he could take a look at the time. After straightening his arms and legs, Thomas turned his head towards the clock only to find that he was already ten minutes late for school! Quickly he rushed to the closet and pulled out his school uniform, brushed his teeth while folding his quilt. Mumbling random words at an amazingly high speed to cool down his nerves, he couldn't help getting chills at the thought of running late on a school day. He had never done that before. Still he took five seconds to look at himself before he walked out of the door. Through the "mirror" he savored a moment at the sight of the label "Punctuality" on the left side of his neck while the feeling of a slight sting went up to his brain. Then he dashed out of the door.

Thomas jumped up on his bike and rode directly towards school. Normally, the sight of all the passers-by on the street would arouse his interest and lead him to take a second look, but he could not this time. On any other day, he would walk slowly to school while skimming the various labels on the bodies of strangers. It had come to an era when labels and "mirrors" prevailed.

People in this world evolved into a species whose body structure was relatively strange compared to the work of nature. They evolved for the need of a more transparent social system. People had their skin made of labels which, different from usual skin, were constantly changed in a modified pattern. The branded words dominating their skin could only be viewed and changed by the people aside from themselves. This period of time went on just fine as people were satisfyingly ignorant of their own personalities, until the invention of "mirrors" crashed into the world with its profound birth. A "mirror" helped the owners of the labels see those words of description branded on their bodies. Though the "mirrors" were cheap, the greatness of self-seeing came at a different price. Ones that looked at themselves through the mirror experienced physical pain which would multiply during the extending time of observing. Half an hour of looking would make a person fall into unconsciousness and further health problems. Actually, the recent invention of the "mirrors" was the cause of Thomas's nightmare that night. Despite all his concerns and worries about the new product, he still bought one into his house, plainly out of curiosity.

By the time Thomas arrived at school, it had been already the end of first period. His arrival was most certainly unwelcome, as the teacher commented Thomas's walking in by, "Mr. Punctuality, you sure are never late. So forgive me for finishing this class before time." Standing at the classroom door, feeling completely ashamed of himself, he was drowned in fear in front of the judging eyes of almost everyone around him. Was he to know that his label of "Punctuality" soon turned into a new one— "Laziness", how much more awful would he had felt?

II

At the dining table, Thomas sat with his usual crew, his best friend Harriet, and two other friends they met newly. Harriet had always been very talkative until very recently she became troubled because of the "mirrors".

After Thomas told her about his nightmare, she finally replied, "How is it that before the 'mirrors' came out we were just fine, but all of a sudden we're all depressed when nothing has really changed? We still see each other the way we always do. Why would we feel so much different about ourselves?"

"Maybe we used to be too ignorant of who we actually are. It might be nice to grasp a more comprehensive view of ourselves." Thomas thought for a while, and said.

"No, Thomas. The labels aren't at all who we are. They are description that others use, how the others see us, and that is not who we actually are." Said Harriet passionately.

However, Thomas was clearly distracted by another boy walking by and neglected her words. The boy, whose face was entirely covered by the label "Coolness", he was named Elliot. Although Thomas saw him every day at school, Elliot's extraordinary label stole Thomas's attention especially on this day. How envying it seemed that Elliot had the label that everyone else was looking to copy! Thomas could not help but expressing, "How easily people's reputation could be stained! It seemed almost impossible to be so perfectly labeled like Elliot. Everyone looks up to him like some god." His voice naturally went up and people around him heard.

Harriet saw his face in a complex expression which seemed to be a mixture of worship, eagerness and jealousy. She bit her lips unintentionally and had a bad premonition.

For Thomas, a plaint was just a plaint until later a girl delicately dressed pulled him out of the hallway when he was walking alone. She dragged him into an empty room where they could not be seen. Thomas looked at her from top to bottom and found her labels extremely perfect, which reminded him of Elliot.

"Thomas, it's nice meeting you. My name is Ursula." She seemed a bit of nervous when talking. "I have something to tell you. I heard you questioning Elliot's perfect labels over lunch⋯"

"Oh, that, I didn't mean⋯" Thomas panicked and immediately denied.

"No, please, I heard what you said and I am turning to you for help." It seemed as if she was about to shed a tear when she continued, "Elliot is not as good as he seems. He had a terrible childhood which built up his violent and grumpy disposition, and on personal occasions Elliot cursed people and even picked up fights."

"What can I do for you, may I ask?"

"He⋯ He's a family friend of mine and I just, I want someone to know about this and help me change him, because, he used to be such a tender friend⋯" Ursula burst out crying.

Out of sympathy, he naturally believed every word she said and promised to offer help.

Thomas brought it up over lunch on the next day. He whispered to his friends and asked them to keep it secret. Harriet listened and stared at Thomas in mistrust. "Are you kidding me? Ursula would tell you about this? Haven't you doubted why she would choose you? You hadn't even met before."

"Because she heard me talking in the diner and she chose to trust my goodness. Maybe she just thought that her friends wouldn't believe her."

Then Harriet's eyes were full of disbelief. "Only you would believe her. Haven't you seen how hypocritical she seemed every time she smiled? Oh, give it a rest, Thomas." Then she walked away.

Little did he know that the labels "Self-esteem" and "Ration" on his right cheek turned into a large word "Vanity" in his best friend's eyes.

III

Suddenly Thomas found himself sitting alone at the dining table. The misery of loneliness matched his depression of learning new negative labels on his body quite well. He looked at himself in the "mirror" for ten minutes the day before and his head ached still this day.

Being weary and exhausted, Thomas saw a person in fancy designer's clothes walking over to him. Before he could start to talk, the person cut in. "Why are you spreading rumors about Elliot?" The person was in rage.

"I'm sorry but I was not. What are you talking about?" The first thought in his mind was to deny, then he came into realization that the incident of Ursula must have been spread by his two new friends at the dining table that day.

The person started to shout, "I am Elliot's mother. Your words have gone everywhere in this school and it has seriously affected his life. How can you say these irresponsible and false things about my Elliot!"

"I didn't start these things. It was Ursula who came to me for help and told me all of this!" Thomas panicked under the staring of people and tried to transfer the blame to someone else, not knowing that it actually made him look guilty in a further degree.

"Do you expect me to trust you? Ursula is the best friend of Elliot, I suppose you don't know? And take a look at her labels. Please, find a more reasonable scapegoat next time if you must have one."

Thomas felt he was trapped in this mess that he didn't mean to cause. Frightened by the condemning eyes of everyone, he still caught the sight of Ursula in the distance. He saw her smiling.

Later, learning that he got a suspension from school, he went home feeling extremely in despair. It hadn't been long until Harriet came to visit, in silence. After seeing how depressed Thomas was, she sighed.

"Harriet, how did I get here?" Thomas opened his strengthless eyes up wide and stared directly into the "mirror". "See? Here on my left cheek, is the new label, 'Liar'. And here, 'Slanderer'. Then this very big one, 'Rudeness'. And⋯And this⋯ This 'Unfriendliness'. Just when I thought 'friendliness' was the only thing I've got." He touched these labels and felt sorry for himself.

Harriet had a long pause then said, "Thomas, you know, I threw away my mirror. I was very depressed when I went through a time knowing how everyone thought about me. But here's the thing, Thomas, this is not how I think about myself. Caring so much about what people who don't understand me think about me is of no use at all. Everyone appears to have flaws whether they like them or not. What people say about you is not you. How people define you is not you. Caring about these labels is not you. Thomas, you need to see that."

The moment Harriet walked out of his room, Thomas collapsed onto his bed. Kindness. Friendliness. Politeness. Self-esteem.

Punctuality. Everything he had once had, did he have it still? Were these labels he actually had? He stood up for a last look at himself in the mirror and he stared into his own image. It was hard and painful for him, physically and psychologically. Could anyone see me under my skin?

Then he smashed the mirror out of his bedroom window.

（作者学校：江西师范大学附属中学）

本文为2018年"北大培文杯"决赛参赛文

4

IT IS TIME TO CONNECT

> There are dark shadows on the earth, but its lights are stronger in the contrast.
>
> ——Charles Dickens

文学是世俗魔法，与当下不可分割。社会现实题材的文章需要写作者有一双犀利的"透视眼"，以拨开纷繁复杂的现象迷雾，直击事物本质。

这一篇篇情怀殷切、针砭时弊的社会题材文章，或聚焦历史变迁，书写个体在时代洪流中的浮沉；或聚焦人类文明，组织最真实的日常生活与全球局势，抨击战争，质问何时打破国家、种族、人与人之间的无形壁垒；或聚焦人性，深刻探讨人性与道德、爱与恨的话题，强调人类对内心良知的反思。

本篇所选文章体现出了文学的多样生态。小作者们深刻的思想见解、精巧的构思，共同构筑了文中富有张力的时代画面。当今国际风云变幻，世界日新月异，但是人性稳固不变。小作者们在对人类历史的反思中和对人类文明的不断探索中，表达了自己的人文情怀和普世观念。

It Is Time to Connect

> **作者的话**
>
> 年十七，好属文，六艺经传皆习之，现学于石门。自诩匹夫而志天下，常谓技不如人而愿学，喜结四方好友，愿虽蜉蝣而有益于世。

E-KEY ARRIVED
—AD SCRIPT OF AN ONLINE SHARE CAR COMPANY

李宇峰

Scene Ⅰ:

A man is trying to get a taxi with his hands waving hard, but he doesn't get one because the taxi passing by is full.

Scene Ⅱ:

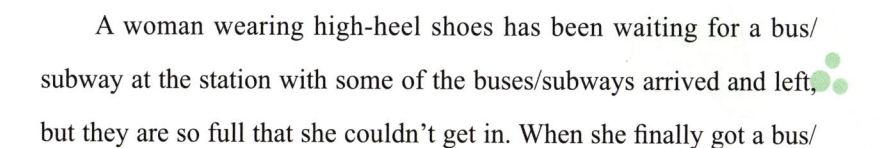

A woman wearing high-heel shoes has been waiting for a bus/subway at the station with some of the buses/subways arrived and left, but they are so full that she couldn't get in. When she finally got a bus/

subway and arrived at another station, there is still a long way to go.

Scene III:

A man is driving his own car, but there is a heavy traffic jam as usual so he is unable to move even a little. At last the cars are free but he finds that his car is out of oil so he has to take some.

Scene IV:

Walking to the nearest A's (company's name) special parking area and looking at a car, a man input the number of the car online, and then he received a key from an e-mail. But it isn't a true key but an electronic one (the e-key), with a sound like: E-key arrived! With the E-key, he sent the signal to the car and opened the doors. Driving the car, the road is unobstructed and broad, and it is very fast to arrive at the place he wants. Just park the car at the nearest special parking area and pay the bill online. The e-key would be sent back automatically.

Sound of commentary (start between the scene III and the scene VI):

Are you still using the crowded and inconvenient buses or subways? Are you still annoyed with the taxi you can't take? Are you still angry with the traffic jam all year round and the not only expensive but also polluted oil? Hurry to use our share car! We have a lot of special parking areas which are absolutely enough for you so you don't need to worry about whether you can find one. All of your cars are using solar energy-water-hydrogen oxygen fuel cell, so there is no oil needed and no pollution. Our computer will collect all the information such as usage time, distance, weight to calculate the price automatically. It's cheap and pretty convenient. Our cars both are safe and can reduce the traffic pressure. Share car, your new way to trip.

(Logo)

(End)

P.S.

1. Emphasize our car's comfortable and beautiful inside.

2. When people are waiting for so long at scene one, two and three, they are quite anxious, try to stress on this point, such as a woman seeing a crowded bus or a man looking at the red light which tells him that his oil box is empty.

3. Using the share car, the man feels happy and cozy. Make it a comparison with other ways. Use the slow-motion.

（作者学校：河北省石家庄市第二中学）

本文为2016年"北大培文杯"决赛参赛文

作者的话

我，一名普通高中生。在校园，或融身于野芳鲜草碧树古木间，聆听自然的萌动；或抒怀于与伙伴的讨论，激扬文字，指点江山；或徜徉于科学海洋，饱饮知识甘泉。

我，一个热爱生活的少年。练习羽毛球、网球，让我强健了体魄，又收获了拼搏后的欣慰与满足；沉醉阅读，令我丰富了阅历，习得客观辩证的思维习惯；自小学习小提琴，让我浸泡在音乐的典雅灵动中，又品尝到持之以恒的艰辛与甘甜。

我，更是一个未来的世界人。我关注着日新月异、风云变幻的世界村。英语为我打开了又一扇世界之窗，阅读令我了解周遭，写作让我抒发己见。携语言的钥匙，我愿认识世界。

THE WALL OF CONSCIENCE HAS BEEN BROKEN DOWN

吴希言

Staring through the dim dust and mist,
Walls, I can see, are standing in front.
In the way of evolution, acting
As the milestones of we human.

I see the original pure garden

In which live Eva and Adam.

It should be without disturbance, tranquilly

Seen the charming blossoms and the solemn fall leaves.

The moment her snow-white fingers stroke the apple,

The moment her rosy lips touch the forbidden,

Boom— the wall of lust broke through the ground,

Yet a wall seems to be broken down.

Crowds gather, crowds separate, as

The wheels of time carry the cart forward.

The evil flame quietly burns,

Scorching the hearts, but no one finds.

Standing on the high tower above the kingdom,

The king looks down at his people.

Just a wave. Just a nod.

Just a game, with flooding blood.

Under the scarlet setting sun,

Shivers in the panic scream.

Boom— the wall of savageness broke through the ground,

Yet a wall seems to be broken down.

Crowds gather, crowds separate, as

The wheels of time carry the cart forward.

The complete darkness secretly extends,

Shadowing the hearts, but no one finds.

It is a desperate desolation—

The colorful rivers dye the massive world,

While the flies eulogize the beauty,

And people live, as if better than ever.

Who can hear the weep of earth the mother?

Who can realize the dazzling colors poisonous?

Boom— the wall of selfishness broke through the ground,

Yet a wall seems to be broken down.

Crowds gather, crowds separate, as

The wheels of time carry the cart forward.

The triumphant troops march arrogantly,

Only heading to the immense abyss.

The human race has been developing up.

The walls have been built and broken down.

Our physical body is full of power,

But who knows the inner world is a deserted hell?

I'd rather have the conscience wall up,

Than the impudent milestones flaunting the ignorance.

The wall of conscience has been broken down,

But I will try to build it up.

（作者学校：广东省中山市第一中学）

本文为2016年"北大培文杯"决赛参赛文

> **作者的话**
>
> 我的书写很糟糕，语文、外语都一样。因为自己没有写作的需求，所以它一直都不是我的兴趣，甚至连工具都算不上，只是偶尔心血来潮蹦几个字罢了。
>
> 说说我和英语的关系吧，其实就一句话：别人学英语，而我是和英语像朋友一样去交流，我和它是朋友关系，以后还可能成为知己。

IT IS TIME TO CONNECT

潘岩

In the modern era we currently live, how do we absorb knowledge effectively and efficiently? Through organs such as eyes, ears and our brains? Using tools and equipment like laptop, smartphones and other electronic devices? I say NO!

Connection is the best way to achieve this goal.

Take a quick look at our history, or rather the human's civilization, then we can draw a conclusion: Connection brings evolution. When ancient people connected themselves to the earth, crops showed up with evolution of living. When the civilization of the west and that of east met and connected to each other, here came the evolution. When E=mc² connected matter to energy, science evolved. The core of evolution is connection.

However, the following question brings us another problem, which is of importance— "How do we connect?" The solution is right in front of us: Break down the wall.

The technology indeed has broken a lot of walls for us even before we realize. As a result, we now possess the capability of doing what our grandparents and the pioneers failed to do, great causes that were supposed to be done decades ago.

Papers broke the wall of time and space, but didn't break the wall of precision. When we are reading books or notes, we may miss details or critical information that may lead us to the truth. However, when we are watching videos and movies, the loss of intelligence becomes less. The wall of precision has been broken down. We can easily identify most of a person by checking his financial checks, reading his personal files and viewing his recorded messages and living tracks without making too many mistakes and wasting a huge amount of time. We can precisely locate a package or a cargo and view its situation whether it is near us or far out through the Internet. We can also learn about an object which is not familiar to us by seeking, collecting and processing tons of relevant information within less time and more understanding with the help of Cortana, Siri, Jexus and so on. Since the wall of precision has been broken down, we can do things more than our imagination.

There is an old saying: "Vision decides success." I don't know whether it is correct. I just know the wall of vision has been broken down. If you want to know more, please read the followings to see how I illustrate my point.

Photos and pictures taken by millions of people in places of the world widen what we can see. Different scenic places and views now can be shared by people of every pieces of the world through Facebook, Twitter, Instagram and friend agenda and other social media. Events can take place under various circumstances and most of those changed into accidents. In the old time, people can only learn from a few of them. But nowadays things are not what they used to be. We can grow up by learning and experiencing more of them to be a better person as well as widen our visions of mind and safety. If we can see more, what could we do? If we can be a better person by paying a smaller price than before, what could happen? If these two add up and emerge, what would the future be? No one can anticipate that since the wall of vision has been broken down.

Can I please ask you fellows? "What is the most valuable thing given by the world?" I don't know your answers, but mine is HUMANITY.

Has the wall of humanity been broken down? Well, at least a part of it has gone. The Berlin Wall is a mark of that. The Berlin Wall used to be a sword cutting Germany in half. At that time, no one believed that wall could collapse, or the sword could be destroyed. Maybe political reasons and military matters resulted in the fall of that, but I believe that humanity should be given much credit to. The people of a country would never want to see their nation fall apart or be separated violently. That is humanity. Today, many companies, new ones, are created due to the commercial system and modern economy, especially the Internet. Some of them like HUAWEI, MEIZU, TAOBAO, ALIBABA and many other companies and corporations established not only based on technology, remarkable geniuses and fortune but also based on humanity. Different people using different tools, having amazing ideas gathered together to do: to challenge, to lead the time and to form the future, which is humanity. I always have faith in the theory—"Wherever there are people, there is humanity." The wall of humanity may not been broken, but part of it has fallen, there is already much we can do so why don't we move right now? Why not proceed in advance? Why not try to connect with our surroundings, again?

In fact, that is all I want to say, I need to say today. But I think I still owe myself another thing, a point for myself— GAMES. Many years spent on games gives me one precious, satisfactory, pleasant and wonderful epiphany. Games broke the wall of me. I got to see other nonexistent or virtual people's lives. Ezio, Sam Fisher, Price, Drake, 47, Chief, Dadin and others. They accompany me for many years till now which grants me the best comfort I can ever have. I am very grateful to them for what they have done for me by breaking down the wall of me.

Thank you for your time. My gratitude is beyond words, my best wishes and heartfelt greetings to you all.

（作者学校：新疆维吾尔自治区乌鲁木齐市第八中学）
本文为2016年"北大培文杯"决赛参赛文

> **作者的话**
>
> 我是一个默默喜爱英语的小城姑娘,有幸参加培文,抱着何妨一试的心态赴京赶考,却收获了这个夏天一朵美丽的惊喜。
>
> 培文为我的高中英语竞赛之旅画上了一个圆满的句号。回首来路,我看到曾经点点滴滴的坚持终究化作了沿路的风景。我记得一篇篇反复朗读、背诵的新概念课文,记得沉浸在英文里的陶醉和笔记本里那些打动过我的英文歌词,在英文名著中时而随着故事情节心绪起伏、时而惊叹于名家老练的笔法和绝妙的构思……厚积薄发,逐渐得出其中真味,用英语开辟了一方属于自己的小小天地,在那里我可以天马行空,纵意驰骋,也可以凝神静气,细细思索,还可以看到别人一语道破我心中表达不出的感想——只言片语中藏着如觅知音的欣喜。

WALLS BETWEEN PEOPLE

张雨菡

The wind was swirling and this cold European air filled in every corner of my lungs. We were in a cramming crowd like penguins in the South Pole whereas we didn't have thick furs to keep us warm like those fluffy creatures. Dad tucked my hand in his. I immediately felt

4 It Is Time to Connect

that I was still safe and sound as if I had been at home although right now we were thousands of miles away from home.

Away from the mosques.

Away from the school where I studied and dad taught.

And away from my dear mom.

She didn't leave home with us and we lost contact shortly after we arrived here. I tugged dad's sleeve. "Daddy, I miss mom. Why doesn't she call me? Doesn't she miss me?" I looked into his eyes which were bouncing, avoiding mine. "She, um, she is busy. Or maybe her phone broke down." I tried to track his eyes but failed. He just turned his head away and said, "Are you hungry now?"

I shrugged. His avoidance confirmed my major concern. Yesterday I overheard his conversation with another man in broken sentences, "a missile bombed⋯ in our neighborhood⋯ lost contact ever since⋯ probably gone." Their voices were not deliberately lowered down because dad, I supposed, thought a seven-year-old kid like me wouldn't understand. But I did. And I did from a long time ago. Dad forgot that being young doesn't mean being a child. We were "children" without childhood.

I drew my hand back. Even though dad was with me, this was no way home. We were far away from home and short of clothes, food, money, jobs⋯ everything. Every day I woke up in this strange, cold place called Europe and stared at that wall for a whole day. Dad told me that as long as we could make it through the wall, we could lead a much more comfortable life as we used to have at home. But the wall stood and the door wouldn't open. There were soldiers guarding it and patrolling around to make sure none of us could go through. Every time they moved, attention shifted to them like sunflowers turning to the sun. People begged for mercy, but were ignored.

I hated the wall. It blocked our way towards a comfortable life and left us here, freezing and starving to death. I couldn't figure out the reason why they couldn't let us in. We could make a living by our own. People around me used to be engineers, professors, businessmen and so on. Dad once told me about the havoc some refugees caused in the city and after that people treated us as if we were viruses, something devastating if caught. I knew there were Muslims that turned into terrorists and started wars and slaughtered innocent people in the name of our religion. People hated them and so did we. They were not real Muslims. The Koran has taught us to treasure peace. They stained our religion we used to be proud of and satisfied their own demands in ruthless ways. I never blamed the soldiers who kept us away. I knew those walls were built by those so-called Muslims who misguided people to view Muslims as terrorists. The walls made of bricks obstructed us to go into those peaceful countries. The invisible walls between people kept others in a safe distance from us. They were afraid to befriend us, employ us or even greet us. Refugees who were lucky enough to cross the borderline still lived under the misunderstanding the mainstream media cast on them, those fluttering rumors dumped on them. They might even find it difficult to become assimilated into the community after settling down for a few years.

Sometimes I wished I could become a giant and thus break the wall down forever. But physical force could never break the invisible ones. We are like an unwanted burden thrown among the UN. And wherever we go, walls have been built in front of us.

Days were gone in a flash. Soon I turned eight. Dad apologized to me that my birthday could not be celebrated as before. "Honey, life is not a fairy tale. But you will always be my little princess." Suddenly I shouted, "No, it is! It is, dad! Look, the wall!" Dad turned back and saw the wall was being broken down by the soldiers who told us the government decided to let us in. Dad burst into tears and held me up to the sky. Everyone was screaming, beaming and hugging each other. The laughter grew louder and louder…

Suddenly, silence.

I rubbed my eyes confusedly and found myself comfortably in bed. I was in China, safe and sound.

I sighed. I woke up and found it was a dream. The walls haven't been broken down and the happiness for the refugees was in vain. I randomly turned on the TV and saw presidents of European countries signing on an agreement to let in the refugees…

（作者学校：安徽省铜陵市第一中学）
本文为2016年"北大培文杯"决赛参赛文

> **┃ 作者的话 ┃**
>
> 风萧萧兮月色悲悯，尘世如烟谁忆？执笔，乱世浮沉，何时，风止尘定。写作，从未能影响这世界分毫，惟是予己心一所安停。笔尖在白纸上探索，许是梦阮口中的练达人情，抑或是浮世黑暗中那一点至光明的向往。培文，于湖光塔影间，为一颗渴盼蓝天的心，营造一个风雨后温暖的巢。

RISING TIDE

张静仪

The tide rises, the tide falls.

He lay in bed, hearing the tide patting on rocks, and slowly closed his eyes…

Ⅰ Birth

The light sound of crying gave life to the long silence outside, honestly speaking, the only sound of tide.

A baby, Alfred was born near the France Western Coast. He grew up, accompanied by the moon and the tide. The name was referred to as hope and brightness.

The story of Santiago impressed on his mind deeply. Alfred even dreamed of fighting with shoals of sharks and becoming admirable among the people in this small town.

II **Adolescence**

Alfred dreamed a lot, but poorly, his work was in a mess. He always wanted to be like Crystal, the No.1 in his class.

In the small school, Alfred only had two friends, Crystal and Chris. Crystal was like her name, loved or even spoilt by her noble family. While Chris lived a poor life, but there was always a big smile on Chris' face.

"How can an orphan be so positive? "Alfred wondered but didn't dare to ask a word.

III **War**

Armies gathered in town and even occupied the tiny school.

"But this doesn't seem to be bad news to us."

Though afraid of the tall and fierce guys, still the three teens chased one another on the coast, laughing and chattering.

Until Alfred found the two dead bodies of his parents and a courtyard filled by soldiers, he was shocked.

Blood mixed up with tide.

Alfred howled to the sky he once gazed at, to the moon shadow he once kissed, to the tide he once slept with, but got no answer.

In the morning tide brought everything away, his home, his happiness, and even his soul.

Ⅳ Separation

Nazi slaughtered everything they met, even the flying birds.

Alfred left the coast where he grew up. Without tide, he felt that there was something elapsed.

Chris and Crystal left, too.

There was nothing now.

Ⅴ Choice

Loneliness filled up Alfred.

Alfred fled into the old house which seemed to have the magic to pull him back.

When he was recollecting the time backward, a different sound appeared out of the tide. Though it sounded slightly, Alfred made sure that there was someone tapping the door.

What he found was a man in blood. He was so much like his father.

To his sympathy, he used some medicine on the blooded man.

But when he found the identity of the guy, he hesitated. Words—"the General of the Nazi army", penetrated his eyes.

Saving him was a betrayal, letting him die was another kind of betrayal, just betraying his deepest heart.

VI Encounter

Tide padded on the stones violently.

Darkness covered everything, including the struggle in Alfred's mind, as well as a gun pointing at him.

He didn't know when the woman came in and stood behind him until something shot into his body and something hot poured out.

Crystal, the girl he admired, and her father lying on the bed killed Alfred.

She glanced at Alfred, left without a word.

VII Imagination

Alfred thought he would die in a couple of minutes and slowly closed his eyes.

Not knowing what had happened later, he woke up on a white bed and found Chris beside.

Alfred crawled up excitedly, finding that it was his friend that saved him a life. To his unexpectedness, Chris joined the French Self-defense Corp.

Even sometimes, he didn't recognize whether this was a dream or reality.

Ⅷ Bottle

Alfred worked under Chris, but both of them treated each other the way they were little.

When Chris commanded, Alfred did at once. Maybe this was where the only difference lay in.

The war continued, though failed, they worked together like just having one heart.

However, when more secrets were divulged to the enemies, something went wrong.

They almost went everywhere together, but there was only one place Chris went alone, taking a tiny bottle with him.

Ⅸ Light

Alfred sat back in the broken house, the moon leaving a shadow of radiance over the coast. Tide rushed as before.

He lost in thought until dazzled by something tiny but shiny in the distance, something unusual, like glass.

The coast was always spotless, with no other mixture, except for blood.

Curiosity pushed Alfred to see what it was.

A tiny bottle, half of which was buried in sand while the top reflected the moonlight.

Then Alfred recognized clearly why the secrets were known to enemies.

X Tide

Alfred led Chris to the coast, the place where they first met.

Memories poured but no words could be said.

They lay on the coast, blood pouring out.

Alfred crawled to the bed which he was born on, leaving a trail of red behind.

Tide rose, taking the gun away, washing what was left on the coast.

And falls.

The moon still shines, the tide will never stop rising.

（作者学校：山西省太原市第五中学）

本文为 2018 年"北大培文杯"决赛参赛文

> **作者的话**
>
> 一次奇妙的燕园之旅,一场与文字的清新邂逅,一段难以言说的不解之缘,一次梦想与坚毅的心中暗藏。不甘于眼前的苟且,那就和着心中的鼓点,因为还有诗和远方。

THE ONLY SURVIVOR

郭奕萱

I

"Ok, everyone, this is C City News. Recently there are four persons that have been murdered by someone in our city. This event has caused chaos on a grand scale and the police have already begun to look into the truth. The only similarity among them is that every one of the four sufferers has a key in their pockets. But the police have no idea of that."

"Wow, it's really a big hit, isn't it?" April said.

"Not exactly, well, I think it's just a small trick." I said with an inadequate smile. But at the same time, a terrible sense appeared in my heart. "There is something horrible happening." I mumbled.

II

Norway.

A winter morning.

"Morning, Andy. Oh, I nearly forget that. Your mail is in the box. Remember to fetch it."

"Okay. I will." I turned over my body and fell asleep deeply again. Suddenly the alarm clock went off disturbing my dream. I woke and sat up just like a zombie, then went straight to the mail box. I took the mail out only to find that there was no name and address on the envelope, but it was really well sealed. With curiosity I opened it. At that moment, I froze with my mouth open. It was so amazing that I couldn't believe it! There was a key, the completely same key like the four murdered persons! I trembled with the cold sweat on my forehead. Does it mean death?

III

"Calm down, Andy. Have you seen the note in the envelope? It says, 'Unless you find the right door which is corresponded with the key, you will die. Or you could choose to wait to go for the hell.'"

"It's a warning. And it means death." I said with no hope in my mind.

"Cheer up, guy. Methods are always more than difficulties."

It was all of a sudden that April reminded me that he mastered a company called Door Doctor which produced doors of high quality.

Therefore, I turned to him.

"Help me search the doors which are corresponded with the shape of the key in the city, please."

"Ok, three days."

IV

Three days later.

"Look, Andy. There are 120 doors being in conformity with the shape all up. What about them?"

"We can't try one by one. To put it another way, we must be positive."

I turned back to my room. This time I froze again. A large number of blood traces appeared on my door which made up a strange triangle. What did it mean? It cast a black cloud in my heart.

V

During the following days I couldn't fall asleep all night. Or sometimes I woke suddenly from a nightmare, yelling "help". But the nightmare reminded me of a fire disaster many years ago. I went on business at that time and lived in a hotel. On a certain night a strange fire burnt the top floor down. Under the critical circumstance, we had no choice but to use the only one elevator at the risk of being swallowed by the fire. But the limit of the elevator was five persons. There were six persons left on the top floor including me. At last a kind girl named Liz volunteered to step out of the elevator. But she herself lost her young life in the horrible fire.

When the memory recovered from the dust of time, I gradually remembered that the four sufferers might be other four ones in the elevator. And there was no denying that I was the fifth one. Someone maybe wanted to kill us to compensate for the dead girl! And it flashed through my head that the triangle made of the blood meant a Greece letter, delta. It meant the fifth one.

VI

I started my car and headed for the old hotel in which I lived many years ago. It was still in use but the top floor vanished in the fire. I stood in the hall just as the event happened yesterday. Taking a deep breath, I went towards the elevator that witnessed the disaster.

Suddenly the little hole on the door of the elevator attracted my eyes. A sense pushed me to take out the key and just at the same time I realized that they corresponded with each other! Then I put the key into the hole carefully.

"Hey! You!" A deep voice said to me.

Then I saw a man in his thirties walking towards me. Tears were filling his eyes, but he still shouted at me. "Because of you five persons, my sister can't see the colorful world anymore! Now I need you to accompany her."

"But wait, sir." I forced myself to cool down. "Your kind sister did volunteer to step out of the elevator. We didn't force her to do that!"

Tears dropped down his cheek and he nodded.

"I know the truth now. Well, it's my entire fault…"

I pat his back and comforted him.

"Since it has been the past, let us forget the hate."

The hooter went off outside the building. It seemed that the police had found out the truth.

VII

Norway.

Winter still.

The sun rises behind the hill far away from my house. It's a completely new day now.

Everyone has their own responsibility, which means that we have the responsibility to think about others just like the kind girl. That day we saved our lives narrowly with the shame. So we have the responsibility to enjoy the colorful world and live better on behalf of the girl.

I'm the lucky one, the only survivor.

[I will dedicate this article to my childhood buddy, Andy.]

（作者学校：河南省安阳市第一中学）

本文为2016年"北大培文杯"决赛参赛文

> **作者的话**
>
> 从笔尖流淌到纸面上的，不仅是对家国情怀的坚守，更是对国际视野的展望。与"北大培文杯"同行，在文学的枫林中拾起最艳红的秋叶，在写作的瀚海里捞出最闪耀的珍珠。青春虽短，却永驻于我们的写作当中。感谢"北大培文杯"，伴我一路走来。

PEOPLE AND LABEL

滕子牧

People create labels then use them.

Yes, we have been using them frequently in the daily life for a long time, especially in today's world of electronic and information, everything seems more convenient to find with a label. We can use them in editing passages, making statistics, even enriching collections.

Making labels for things can not only be tidy, but also save time. Everything is just in order since we follow the labels. But something that isn't so good happens, when people add labels to each other.

Like a price tag, everyone in others' eyes can be just a label with several lines of descriptions. Such as a good kid, an extremely strict teacher, or maybe another kind of people with another adjective word.

It can also be about achievements, history behaviors and personalities.

Labels of people cannot be sorted by the Internet, for sure, since there're so many of them, and it's hard to tell which one is better. But still they can simply be put into two boxes: the good ones, and the bad ones. Or in other words, the colorful and shining ones, and the ones full of spots and disadvantages.

And there the problem comes. As time goes by, people can zoom these labels without sense or not on purpose. Good things turn better, bad things turn dirtier. The labels seen by others become the people themselves. No matter how great they actually are, they become dirty due to their labels. The more famous the person is, the stronger the glue is to connect him and his labels. Gradually labels become people, and people are labels.

Do we ever forget that although it might be one's own behavior that leads to a label, it is us that actually create it?

Think about this. People are no longer living their lives. They are modelling after labels. If you see a good kid who should be in a pair of glasses as thick as a bottom of a beer bottle, turning pages and writing letters or numbers all day in the classroom, but today he is playing soccer on the playground, shouting, falling over, ruining his quietness of character, what will you think? Will the first thing occurs to you be feeling strange or happily accepting? So, does our main character have enough bravery to make this change with those face-to-face questioning people even though he wishes to change from the bottom of his heart? These answers are uncertain.

What is even worse, a famous star doing a lot of charities and donating much, may be questioned for some little bad fake things made up by people who want to attack him, and thus lose fame forever. A person out of prison will be questioned everywhere no matter whether he had made up his mind to become a brand-new person. Bad labels are always hard to remove. Maybe everyone has offered efforts to this society, hoping to remove labels that affect them adversely. But most of the time, the only thing they get is just an experience of saying "No, you can't." No way to run, nowhere to hide, you are here and labels are here. Please forgive me for not being optimistic, but the fact is here. The relationship among people, society and label, came into being since the ancient time.

At least we have got the opportunities ourselves.

Sticking labels to books could be a relaxing job on weekends. But things go differently when it comes to people. So, what I want to say isn't to stop making labels on people right now, it's about how. The judgement should be from people's hearts, as the saying goes. We should make labels based on facts, not on previous ones in case a wrong one grows bigger. We shouldn't think we have an absolute right to judge people, and once we have to, we should only follow a person's intention, and judge with the law and moral, not from other's word. If the labels have existed, we should consider the change over time, and edit them. People are changeable, and changeful, so are the labels.

From another perspective, if we are given labels which seem bad and wrong, we need to try to change the situation, to tell those label-makers that they are wrong, to show the public and keep the belief that finally there will be a day everyone can get sharper eyes and brighter mind. Then maybe the story will change its end. Others happily accept that the child is not a nerd, but an outgoing hard-working and athletic child.

People create labels. People use labels. People judge according to themselves and are judged by themselves. Using themselves wisely, people can build a better labelled society.

（作者学校：吉林省吉林市第一中学）

本文为 2018 年"北大培文杯"决赛参赛文

It Is Time to Connect

> **┃作者的话┃**
>
> 我是一名高中生，居住在西南地区一座三四线城市。和这本书里的许多作者一样，现时的我正在准备本年度的高考，"紧张而兴奋"。
>
> 然而，无论学业多么繁重、时间怎样紧张，按我个人理解，日常的文学熏陶还是必不可少的。除去那些功利的所谓前途、情怀和作文分，文学之于你我这样的普通人，实与个人的素养、内涵乃至道德水平密切相关。
>
> 这一论断看起来也许有些虚伪造作，但是生活现实却很能支持这一观点：有人光鲜亮丽却出口成脏，也有人"指点江山"但举止下流；有人谈吐不俗且文雅高尚，也有人讷言敏行而藏秀于心。细加思考，我认为，这些行为教养差异应源于某人所处的日常环境，而文学的存在与否，则是塑造这一环境的重要因素。

DO LABELS WORK?

柯思云

Republic of Utopia is now introducing a brand-new system in its customer market in order to protect the privilege of customers and strengthen food safety. A new electronic system will be used to track all the food supplies selling in supermarkets, convenient stores and so on. In a nutshell, an electronic label must be attached on every item that is to be eaten, and the label must be readable by the phones using NFC technology. The data like LOT number, Expiration date or Producer will be stored in a small chip inside the label.

Utopian Senate has just passed a resolution, an Act about the food label, after a long-term debate. It is critical that, the Law not only makes it necessary to store normal data in the chip, but also requires some other data. For example, a tag must also show the possibility of cancer-leading by eating a bag of chips, or the estimated weight-gaining after eating one-pound beef. These data are analyzed by computers and a customer with a smartphone can read them from the E-label of food, so he/she can shop wisely and eat healthily.

All right, Utopians are those who care about their health. Utopian citizens gratefully accepted the new act. And all the food supplies in the country have attached E-labels within 3 months. People start to scan the labels before purchasing. It's reported that the number of hospital-admitted patients who ate bad food is reducing after the 6 months' using of the new system.

Citizens are happy to find the new way to diet healthily. All in all, the food label system is efficient, just scan the tag, and the smartphone will calculate its healthy aspects, so you can easily control your calories, salt or fat. However, some voices against the law begin to spread after 8 months.

Firstly, the producers, they claim that the labels with chips are a little pricy so their profits were decreasing. And then the sellers, they

It Is Time to Connect

find the average time the customers spend in their stores is much longer than before, because they will scan for the health info and calculate eagerly. That makes their grocery full of people and their staffs can be so busy in rush hours.

Finally, some customers also show their disagreement. Before the labels were introduced, they ate happily, although a little unhealthy, as they could not get the analyzed nutrition info. After the using of electronic labels, they began to know some nutrition facts of their favorite snacks and started to avoid them or eat with terror. But the point is, is it really important to know such information like "0.01% possibility of lung-cancer"? It definitely gives enough medical warnings but the information makes customers worry too much about their health unnecessarily.

However, most citizens find it vital to be healthy at that time, so that they decide not to stop the critical law. Indeed, Utopian House of Representative even published a new act to promote the E-label. Using labels is strictly required by Law and incorrect information analyzation is punishable by fine. Besides, not attaching E-labels is a crime under newly-edited Food Safety Law.

So, Utopians continue to use E-label system, scanning each item and calculating with patience. Though the smart tags are pricy, they believe health is the most important.

Months after months, finally, Utopians get something strange. The so-called "unhealthy" food cannot be seen easily in most groceries, as people won't purchase because of the "high-in fat/salt" info given by the E-labels. That's true that eating much junk food is unhealthy, but giving terrifying information directly to customers also causes some mental problems.

Moreover, the illnesses caused by expired food are surely decreasing. But other serious diseases like cancers and brain blooding which are believed to be caused by unhealthy diet, are not seen to significantly decrease. It shows that E-labels are not so helpful to reduce health problems.

In that case, there are also more Utopians who think it's unnecessary to continue to use the advanced electronic labels. So, the President signed an administrative order to pause the using of label system.

Citizens are happy to find there are no more Food Safety Labels to scan. They are not worried about the analyzed food data anymore and are able to eat with happiness again.

In the end, Utopian Supreme Court declares that it is against the Constitution to ask grocery to attach E-label on their items. The previous act is also modified now. Pricy electronic labels are no longer required. The new law just asks producers to use bigger fonts to print "Necessary and Basic" information on their products.

It's unnecessary to analyze too much. What we need is just the basic information that is closely related to the central point of matters. Reading directly a few simple necessary pieces of info like EXP, NET or Permission, is better than analyzing complex sources in that situation. The more you know, the more worried you will be.

It's not just a story or joke happening in the so-called "Republic of Utopia". It's sometimes the truth in our real life. You can easily find several diet Apps annoying you with plenty of "Unhealthy

Alerts". Situation is more serious in medical field, especially the online medicine. There are now some medical websites diagnosing illness according to symptoms, and visitors are there to check themselves. However, it's just like the labels in my story, their analyzations are complex but not deep. In that case, the "health tips online" does not really benefit us but just puzzles the patients.

It's true that a simple "label" is not an answer to complicated issues. It's the real knowledge and awareness that matter.

（作者学校：四川省泸州高级中学）
本文为 2018 年"北大培文杯"决赛参赛文

| 作者的话 |

对于写作，我从未刻意总结。从人类结绳记事开始，记录就已经成为人类的本能。

我曾惊异于自己的构思，现在回顾，仍有那种一口气写完后酣畅淋漓之感；又感叹于写作是现代社会的最后私人空间，深夜孤独时，放下手机，用文字记录下彼时的想法。

无穷的远方，无数的人们，都和我有关。

所以，各位人类观察者，请不要放下手中的笔——那是战士的武器。我跌下悬崖，于是看见繁星满天。

COUNTDOWN

刘笑语

"Five little ducks went out to play;

Over the sea and far away;

Mother Duck said quack, quack, quack;

But only four little ducks came back⋯"

"Emily, stop repeating your stupid and boring song. I've eaten that lost duck, haha." a woman yelled, "Come on. I'm going to teach you numbers from six to ten."

4 It Is Time to Connect

Emily rushed to her mother. Children at her age were always thirsty for something new.

"Open your left hand and then your right hand. Count your fingers and follow me, six, seven, eight, nine… ten!"

After some practice, Emily had already got the hang of counting numbers from six to ten.

"Mama, what if I count them upside down, like ten, nine, eight, seven, six…" Emily asked with curiosity, as if she had discovered a new continent.

"Oh no, stop it, stop it. You can't count like this. I mean… 'Count' means to say numbers in the correct order. You order… how to say this… is not correct."

"Why, mama? I just count it in a different way." Emily seemed frustrated and confused.

"Well, my good girl. I just know if you do things against ordinary rules, you will be punished by them." The mother tried her best to meet her daughter's question.

"Them? Who?"

"The government, the society, the law…"

My friends, when your reading comes here, you must be very confused. It's my fault that I didn't introduce Emily and her mother first. Emily and her mother are in a different world. I don't know where it is, but it does exist. That case always happens. Last month, I made a trip there, which was weird and interesting.

I went there by Tamino, a special boat only used by the local. When I got aboard, every passenger was sitting seriously, yes, seriously. I felt a little awkward, so I sat down as quickly as I can. Nevertheless, after a while, I stand up to see the view outside the window. Then the most embarrassing thing happened: Everyone stared at me, as if I was doing something really strange.

The captain came over, "Behave yourself!" He shouted.

I sat down slowly and asked the person who sat next to me. His name was Jack.

"Our laws don't allow people walking around any transport tool." Jack explained.

"Why? If I want to see the scene outside⋯"

"Then, there is no rule. In our country, if you are in someplace, you must do the certain things." Jack interrupted me.

After the conversation with Jack, I came to learn this special country.

Jack was a student in senior high school. He said it was hard to be a good student especially if you were majored in arts, because the correct answer was only one. For example, if the question was about your idea or attitude towards a historical revolution, you couldn't answer your opinion, but the opinion from the textbook, or the teacher. In other words, if your answer was a little different from the correct answer, you would be ranked as "C" or "D" or even lower.

The government set walls. They set a high wall between themselves and their southern poor neighbor. They set Internet walls to keep their civils away from other countries. How poor those people were!

I once talked to a landlord who owned plenty of fields.

"Don't you wonder what the outside looks like?"

It Is Time to Connect

"Not at all. I heard that people outside don't obey rules. They rush here and there. They do what they want to do! That's crazy! The world is out of order."

"What will happen if a man breaks the 'law'?" I asked.

"They will get mental treat and be sent to the prison. Anyway, if one of my workers become abnormal, he will do harm to my crops." the landlord answered firmly and loudly.

"How about the LBGT? Do you think they are 'abnormal'?"

"Of course! Those limp-wristed are abnormal and dirty. I can't stand!" The landlord seemed surprised for my obvious question.

The country had its certain rules: Women first, men second; colored people first, white people second; minority first, majority second. It was discriminate, but no one stood out to fight against it. The freedom of speech was the last thing the country cared.

My dear friends, when you are reading this paragraph, you've already done my article. Abrahan Linkin said, when people's right of voting is limited, one way or another, it will be released. Jack, Emily and Emily's mother had something in common. They dared not to stand out and fight against it. So, their world was counting down.

At the same time, you feel familiar when you read their stories, because these things also happen around us. Standing silently by unfair stuffs makes us all fall victims.

"Ten, nine, eight, seven, six…" Time still lost. Stop it or not, it's up to you.

（作者学校：河南省郑州市第四中学）

本文为2017年"北大培文杯"决赛参赛文

作者的话

写作的出发点是自身，终点却在他人。每次我写完一些零散的段落，第一件事是与好友分享，看他们如何解读，是否能从中得到一丝洞见。我始终认为，只对自己有意义的文字并不能算好的作品。因此，对于为了博人眼球而陌生化处理文字的举动，我一直不认同，并以此不断警醒自己。正如有人说，若你无法用简单的语言讲解一门学问，是因为你并没有真正了解它。对于生活这门尽管因人而异、仍大有共性的学问而言，这种说法同样适用。因此，如果我浅薄的文字能给予读者一些思考，于我便已经足够。

TEN COUNTS

桂嘉雨

I am the best news commentator of history. I believe in it without even the slightest doubt. You ask me why? Because I do understand how much the ten counts weigh before I begin my live show.

Tik-Tok.

Only god knows what I'm thinking about during those ten seconds.

Sometimes the ten seconds are easy to pass. You just have to clear your throat, pretend a fantastic smile you've ever had, bring out your charisma, and try your very best to make yourself sound nice.

While sometimes things get complicated, you get panic, and the ten seconds become the heavy drum beats thumping with your heart.

Oh yes, that's because you want to make every second of your show counts. You are dying to prove yourself that you deserve the well-paid position and more importantly, you have the capability to shoulder the responsibility of your career.

Wow, that's too much of it. Let's get back to my story.

I had to say that I used to be a perfect news commentator once, for I never said one inappropriate word, which meant I never criticized one certain party or one certain event outside my duty. I simply did my job pretty well, and I played the game completely inside the rules.

In this case, the ten counts seemed like a precious break before I started my daily routines. I felt incredibly great, actually.

"Attention, please. All the departments stand by. Let's start to roll." The voice of my executive producer came through the earphones.

"Ten counts!" The beautiful voice continued.

Got it, Madam.

"Ten!" I blinked a little bit for I didn't get a good sleep last night.

"Nine!" I changed the way I sat on the easy chair to make myself comfortable.

"Eight!" I put on my symbolic smile.

"Seven!" I cleared my throat once again. Listen, that's the 30-million-dollar voice.

"Six!" My mind started wandering. Today's news was shallow but definitely interesting and attractive. The audience rating was guaranteed for sure, which meant my salary was guaranteed as well. Lovely.

"Hey, are you all right?" said my lovely executive producer.

"Absolutely." I answered, casually.

"Then good." A normal check-up conversation. But to me, it sounded a bit frustrated.

What was going on out there?

I swore to God that I cared not because she was my girlfriend. No. I cared because she was my executive producer! Mine!

…Well, fine. It was because she was my girlfriend indeed.

But anyway, right now, I didn't have time to figure it out. Maybe I could do that later.

"Good evening, this is the Great News Studio and I'm your man, Sam Ginsburg. Here is some interesting news that you may want to know about."

"…with the release of iPhone 7, every Apple store in the corner of each block shows a majestic view of the queue. Some crazy fans even put up a tent to get the newly released Apple product as soon as possible…"

"…this is Sam Ginsburg. I'll see you tomorrow."

Done. Applause in the room. Everyday situation, it was nothing to talk about. But it always gave me some sort of feelings that there was something missing in the applause—something important.

"Good job." said Nika, my executive producer plus my cute girlfriend.

"Thanks." I laid a kiss on her forehead. Then the unfinished

It Is Time to Connect

conversation came to me.

"Hey, darling, why did you seem frustrated before? I mean, it's kind of, not your style." I asked carefully.

No response. Silence in the air. And embarrassment spread.

After a few seconds, she looked me in my eyes.

"Sammy my dear, I'm just saying⋯ Do you really think this is a show that you would like to spend your whole career life on?" She answered, frowning with a bitter smile.

And this question struck me dumb.

Oh man, that's exactly what I'm afraid of being asked about.

What I am doing right now is not, apparently, the thing that I would like to devote myself to.

As a newsman, I know exactly what I am supposed to do.

The news I am commenting on is interesting indeed, but unfortunately, it is anything but meaningful.

It's just not enough.

In this world, in every hour of every day, things happen. Good things happen, and terrible things happen as well.

It always feels good to know about the good ones. But honestly, what we really need to know is the truth itself. Is the world as incredible as you see it on TV or hear it on the radio? Everyone has the fundamental right to see it themselves.

What about the poverty, the endless war, those food-deprived kids, the norm of gun violence in some of the districts, and the appalling drug-related crime rate in some seemingly blessed countries?

Do you know what is hidden behind those hilarious soap operas, funny comedies, and even news channels that are supposed to be the very place closest to the reality, but are actually not?

Do you know why some countries are dramatically high in GDP while having the largest population of extremely poor people?

It's because 90% of the wealth is held by only 1% of the whole population and the social welfare system still has a long way to go to ensure the basic rights of the majority instead of maintain the benefit of the power holders.

These are the straight facts.

These are the messages that are deep in our heart, we are dying to know about them because at the end of day, maybe we are unable to do anything to change them, at least we can be sure about one single thing— we are living a real life, and we can say to ourselves— welcome to the real world.

However, it seems that we get caught in a dilemma.

As for the audience, sometimes, we are just afraid to hear those awful and terrible tragedies and always favor the good. We keep lying to ourselves that the world is perfectly fine and everything around us is exactly what it's supposed to be.

We don't want the insecurity and the unpredicted factors of the society. To comfort our fragile heart, we'd rather not hear them.

As for us newsmen, our salary is strongly connected to the audience rating of our show. Meanwhile, some sensible topics are never allowed to be over commented. We have our boss to look out for; our life and even our family's life to take care of and obeying those rules is undoubtedly the No. 1 principle to keep us safe in this ecosystem .

It Is Time to Connect

But, come on, man.

This is not what we exist for.

We choose to be a newsman not because we want to end up like a coward.

Ten counts can sometimes be heavy.

It means we dare to offer the truth, to offer our own voice on certain issues and also let the truth speak for itself.

Responsibilities are the nickname of the risks.

We could have taken on the responsibilities and we could have done something historic and meaningful, for that is exactly what a newsman does.

The question is: are you willing to do it?

This time, I'm sitting on my easy chair, feeling uneasy.

"Attention, please. All the departments stand by."

My heart is beating harder.

"Ten!" Am I going to lose my audience?

"Nine!" Will this topic be allowed to talk about?

"Eight!" What if my boss gets completely mad at it?

"Seven!" Am I going to lose my job as a newsman forever?

"Six…" Am I…

Oh god.

You know what, whatever.

Come on, Sam Ginsburg, act like a real man. Get it together and do your real job.

"Are you ready, Sammy?" The beautiful voice is coming through my earphones.

"Absolutely."

I take a really, really deep breath.

（作者学校：重庆南开中学）

本文为 2017 年"北大培文杯"决赛参赛文

作者的话

作为一名热爱文学的理科生，我爱好阅读、写作，并在其中获得极大的愉悦。在阅读中，我了解未知的世界；在写作中，我明晰自己的内心。

我性格开朗活泼，兴趣爱好广泛，大胆梦想，脚踏实地，忠于现实。在英语方面略有所长，曾任学校广播站"每日英语"栏目的主播，担任过校运动会和2015年石家庄市模拟联合国精英峰会的主持人。希望在未来，我能不断丰富自己，用文字、声音表达自我，感动世界。

WELCOME TO THE NEW AGE

周雨旸

The Wall has been broken down.

Congresswoman Julia Worthing always knows that such a day would come, after all, it's what she has fought for so long.

More than three decades ago, unwilling to free their slaves and end their rule, the aristocrats built the Wall to separate themselves from the free folks who work to earn their own bread.

It was at that time that Julia fled from her parasitical family to join the free folks. She believed in freedom, democracy and equality as she still does now. So her family's lifestyle and horrible behaviors repulsed her. Therefore without hesitation, she joined her comrades and left everything from her past behind, including her family name, and has since then spared no effort to bring the Wall down.

Now the people are raving and cheering in the streets, and those who were once enslaved are being introduced to new homes and jobs. Julia has never experienced such a joyful moment.

Time has come for her to meet the nobles who have just lost their privilege, or as she prefers to call them, leeches. She knows that her own family would be among them, but she remains unsure about whether she should reclaim them. Julia walks into the grand City Hall alongside her fellowmen at a steady pace and is seated in the center with the former aristocrats on her left and representatives of the former slaves on her right.

The mayor mounts the platform and starts to speak: "Brothers and sisters, today, we are here to witness the doom of an old age, and the birth of a new era!"

Julia feels somehow compelled to tilt her head and look for her family.

"The Wall, which has marked a darker time, is now broken down!"

She found him, the man who used to be her father before she denied him, looking much older than she remembered, sitting in the front row with the same frigid and grim look on his pale and wrinkled face, the same look that she loathed so much when young.

It Is Time to Connect

"From this day, no more oppression, no more violence, peace and prosperity shall always endure!"

He saw her, too. Julia knows by the slight tremor of his face. Surprisingly, she found no other family members with her father.

"In the name of freedom and equality, by the power of the city…"

The man that gave her life turns his head to look at her and she suddenly feels as if there were butterflies in her stomach.

"I now bestow you, the right of citizenship! Now you may rise as lawful citizens of our city!"

Every living soul in the hall rises, and Julia knows that all the others who are not here are rising elsewhere.

After the ceremony, Julia makes her way through the crowd to the old man she hardly recognizes. Closer up, she finds him looking even older and frailer.

"Congresswoman Worthing." he greeted her dryly.

"Citizen von Reuental."

"It's citizen Reuental now." he answers in a hoarse voice, "All the inequalities are gone, including 'von's in last names."

"Yes, you're right, citizen. How are you and how's your family?"

"I am alone without family." He answered succinctly.

—"I'm sorry to hear, citizen."

"You shouldn't be." he says, "They lost their lives holding on to the past age, a doomed age."

She feels a lump in her throat, "But I'm sure you must have family elsewhere, don't you?"

"I have a daughter, no, I had a daughter who foresaw all this long before I did and fought for what she believed." There was a glimpse of pride in his eyes and Julia managed to catch it. "Alas, I have no idea whether she'll take me back before my time, I haven't got long, you see."

"May I ask if you share her beliefs now, citizen?"

"I do, I do now. The world rolls on by, and the future is brighter each day. I'm happy to have contributed to the making of it."

Julia suddenly realizes who the mysterious man on the other side of the Wall and helped them was, the evidence was there, and now she finally knows.

"Then I'm sure she would, with open arms."

"Thank you, Congresswoman Worthing."

She replies by stepping up to hug him, and as she does so she feels the wall she built in her heart crumbling down.

"Welcome to the new age, father." She whispered into his ear.

"You too, daughter." And she received a kiss from him on the forehead of which sweetness she knows that only belongs to the new age.

（作者学校：河北省石家庄市第二中学）

本文为2016年"北大培文杯"决赛参赛文

作者的话

　　我是一个兼具理性与感性的人——目光犀利，针砭时弊，说理较真无人可比，有时又会被小细节深深打动而不能自已。我又是一个有着奇思妙想的人——从小便不甘随波逐流，总是以富有创意的奇特目光看待世间万物。正因此，文学成了我的知音。在文学的殿堂里，我体验到逻辑的魅力，为一针见血的语言叫好，也曾"临文嗟悼，不能喻之于怀"。文学千变万化，给我无限思考与无数灵感，给我突破陈规成说的勇气。文学的载体，是语言。在接触各国文学的同时，我也痴迷于它们的语言——我爱汉语的历史悠久、博大精深，爱英语的流畅清新、参差多态，爱法语的雍容华贵、浪漫多情……每一种语言和文学的背后，都是一种独特的文化。我愿与语言文学相伴，去探索世界各个角落多姿多彩的文化。

THE TRACK OF HISTORY

李雅婕

"The tide rises, the tide falls." wrote Henry Wadsworth Longfellow.

　　Throughout history, poets all over the world like to compare history to a river coursing constantly or an ocean with tide rising and falling.

Therefore, in my opinion, Longfellow's word can also be considered as a description of history.

I

Indeed, the tide rises, the tide falls.

Some civilizations survived, others disappeared.

Some people went down in history, others were buried unknown…

The Greek civilization made advances in various fields, such as philosophy, mathematics, art and architecture. Democracy and humanism were also parts of the essence of this civilization.

However, where is it exactly? Why has it become an afterglow? What, or who, made this great civilization a shadow of its former self?…

During the 15th century, there was a long-drawn-out war between France and England, which lasted for nearly 100 years.

At the beginning, the French fought hard, but still lost many battles. The English snatched many parts of the French territory, and claimed that they would surely made France part of England.

The French had nothing left to lose. France was sinking into the Slough of Despond.

That was when the savior, Jeanne d'Arc (Joan of Arc), came into the sight of the French people. She was born a village girl, who didn't even know how to read or write. However, to everyone's surprise, she was talented in handling battles. She successfully cheered up the soldiers, gained victories wherever they went and recaptured many areas lost to England.

The French were proud of her; the English were afraid of her. She was recognized by the French as "la Pucelle d'Orléans" (the Virgin of Orleans).

She was believed to lead France to glory, when she lost the battle in Compiègne and was captured by enemies. Then, in front of the French, she was burnt at the stake—the English set fire, leaving this 19-year-old heroine screaming and struggling helplessly in flames⋯At last, she ended up in ashes.

Whose fault was this?

……

The tide rises, the tide falls.

Nothing can remain on the top forever.

Where there is prosperity, there is depression.

These are what history tells us.

II

However, the poet Longfellow didn't tell us the whole truth.

The tide falls, but it shall rise again.

The Greek civilization never died. It melted into many other civilizations and, during the Renaissance, regained its status. It became the ideological weapon of the bourgeoisie. As far as I know, it is still influencing many Western countries and even the whole world.

As for Jeanne d'Arc, although she was put to death then, her spirit made the French moved. Therefore, the French united to keep fighting, and eventually they won. The long-awaited victory came to France, which resulted in the English fleeing back to their tiny island.

The tide falls, but it shall rise again.

The prosperity won't last, neither will the depression.

When we are at our worst, which might be the time when we can fight back and get back on our feet— "It's not until you fall that you fly." goes the song *Dream It Possible*.

These are also what history tells us.

III

The tide rises, falls and rises again, which forms the track of history.

All these vicissitudes are like the tides: we individuals are just fragile straws floating and sinking…

But that's not to say that we can only swim with the tide. Some people say, "Everything in life is fated." Well, I think this kind of remark is just an excuse for their passivity.

Just think: why does the tide rise and fall? You may say that it's because the waves are pushing and pulling each other. But you forget one thing—the wind!

The opportunities are the wind.

Just like the wind can change the motion of the waves, the opportunities can change the course of our lives. So, why miss them?

As for those who would rather believe that their destinies are fixed, they give up at the very beginning, letting the opportunities pass by. In this fierce-competition society, they are just too passive to bother to survive the race.

While there's no guarantee that we can all realize our dreams and change the world, one thing is for sure—if we seize the opportunities and fight hard, we might succeed, changing the course of our lives and even the history, even though we don't realize it!

The track of history might seem unchangeable, but, remember, the last thing we should do is to swim with the tide.

Even if we can't change the world, we should never give way to passivity, nor should we attribute everything to the twists of fate. At least, we can make ourselves unique individuals, instead of fading into the crowd.

（作者学校：湖南省长沙市长郡中学）

本文为2018年"北大培文杯"决赛参赛文

附录

2016年"北大培文杯"英语创意写作大赛题目

初赛题目

题目1：A secret that cannot be told.

题目2："No. Precious human, you are not the last," he said in a soft, compassionate tone, "you are the first."

This sentence must be the last sentence of your writing.

决赛题目

题目1：The wall has been broken down.

围绕这句话展开联想与思考，创作一篇文章，题目自拟，文体与字数不限。

题目2：You received a key in the mail.

围绕这句话展开联想与思考，创作一篇文章，题目自拟，文体与字数不限。

2017年"北大培文杯"英语创意写作大赛题目

初赛题目

在两道开放性命题中任选一题，文体不限，要求不超过800单词。

题目1：The world in a drop of water.

题目 2: Write a scene that takes place immediately after a tragedy. Don't mention the tragedy.

决赛题目

题目 1: There's an island where all lost things end up. Today, you wake up, cold and wet, on the beach of that island⋯

围绕这句话展开联想与思考，创作一篇文章，题目自拟，文体与字数不限。

题目 2: Ten, nine, eight, seven, six⋯

围绕这句话展开联想与思考，创作一篇文章，题目自拟，文体与字数不限。

2018年"北大培文杯"英语创意写作大赛题目

初赛题目

在两道开放性命题中任选一题，题目自拟，文体不限，要求不超过800单词。

题目 1: Who would you say has influenced your generation the most?

题目 2: What do young people worry about?

决赛题目

以下任选一题，请在大赛专用稿纸上写作，比赛时间为150分钟。

题目 1: 请就 label 这个词思考并展开联想，创作一篇作品，题目自拟，文体和字数不限。

题目 2: "The tide rises, the tide falls." ——Henry Wadsworth Longfellow

请以此句作为文章开头，展开联想，创作一篇作品，题目自拟，文体和字数不限。

图书在版编目（CIP）数据

写给未来的自己. 第2季,"北大培文杯"全国青少年英语创意写作大赛优秀作品 / 刁克利, 高秀芹主编.—北京：中国人民大学出版社, 2019.6
ISBN 978-7-300-26974-0

Ⅰ.①写… Ⅱ.①刁… ②高… Ⅲ.①英语–作文–选集 Ⅳ.①H319.4

中国版本图书馆CIP数据核字(2019)第092178号

写给未来的自己

"北大培文杯"全国青少年英语创意写作大赛优秀作品·第2季
刁克利　高秀芹　主编
Xiegei Weilai de Ziji

出版发行	中国人民大学出版社		
社　　址	北京中关村大街31号	邮政编码	100080
电　　话	010-62511242（总编室）	010-62511770（质管部）	
	010-82501766（邮购部）	010-62514148（门市部）	
	010-62515195（发行公司）	010-62515275（盗版举报）	
网　　址	http://www.crup.com.cn		
经　　销	新华书店		
印　　刷	天津中印联印务有限公司		
规　　格	170mm×240mm　16开本	版　　次	2019年6月第1版
印　　张	17 插页2	印　　次	2019年6月第1次印刷
字　　数	189 000	定　　价	48.00元

版权所有　　侵权必究　　印装差错　　负责调换

人大社青少年写作书目

中国人民大学出版社一直致力于为青少年出版充满创意的写作书,激发孩子的写作思路,让孩子在写作中发现自我、表达自我,同时学习写作技巧,提高写作水平。

写作不只是写作文,它是一种充满想象力的创作,能够极大地拓展人的思维和表达能力,更是一种可以伴随孩子一生的技能。这里有通过画画启发创意思维的《写写画画故事书》,有美国获奖作家系统讲授写作方法与技巧的《写作大冒险》和《小作家手册》,有儿童文学作家带来的《作文课》,有写作大赛名师的课堂再现《丁丁老师创意作文课》……在这里,你能找到孩子喜欢读的写作书。希望人大社写作书不仅能帮孩子学到写作技巧,还能让孩子真正地爱上写作。

书名	作者	出版日期	介绍
《写写画画故事书》(套书五册,赠日记书)	白铅笔	2018年7月	适读年龄:6~9岁。孩子的第一套创意写作启蒙书,让孩子创作出属于自己的绘本故事。
《写作大冒险——惊喜不断的创作之旅》	[美]凯伦·本克	2018年10月	适读年龄:9~18岁。来自美国的超酷创意写作书,可以撕、可以写、可以画、可以玩。
《小作家手册——故事在身边》	[美]维多利亚·汉利	2019年2月	适读年龄:9~18岁。获奖作家为你揭开写作的秘密,你也能成为一名真正的小作家。
《丁丁老师创意作文课——教你写出有个性的作文》	丁丁老师	2018年10月	适读年龄:9~12岁。写自己、写家人、写游记、写场景、写生活,告别套路,教你写出与众不同的味道。
《丁丁老师创意作文课——教你写出会思考的作文》	丁丁老师	2018年10月	适读年龄:9~12岁。写推理、写变形故事、写说明文、写议论文,让你的作文会呼吸,写出自己独特的思考。
《写作魔法书——28个创意写作练习,让你玩转写作》(修订版)	白铅笔	2019年6月	适读年龄:9~15岁。好玩的创意写作练习,你的笔一写就停不下来。写作的魔法就藏在你的脑袋里,快来试一试!
《写作魔法书——让故事飞起来》	[美]加尔·卡尔森·莱文	2014年6月	适读年龄:9~15岁。纽伯利奖获奖作家分享写作秘密,帮你找到绝佳的故事创意。
《作文课:让创意改变作文》	谭旭东	即将出版	适读年龄:9~15岁。贴近中小学生生活的写作课,教你把创意用到写作中。
《写写画画日记书》	白铅笔	即将出版	适读年龄:6~9岁。孩子爱画爱写的日记书,有趣的引导创意多多,让孩子爱上写日记。
《成为小作家》	李君	即将出版	适读年龄:9~12岁。语文名师手把手教你写作,写出自己独一无二的作品。

书名	作者	出版日期	介绍
《少年未来说·第1季》	曹文轩 高秀芹	2019年6月	适读年龄：6～12岁。"北大培文杯"全国青少年创意写作大赛优秀作品（第1季），展现青少年天马行空的想象力和精妙灵动的文字水平。
《写给未来的自己·第2季》	刁克利 高秀芹	2019年6月	适读年龄：10～18岁。"北大培文杯"全国青少年英语创意写作大赛优秀作品（第2季），用英语展现创意与写作，向未来出发。
《北大清华学长的写作黑科技》	《意林》编辑部	即将出版	适读年龄：12～18岁。北大、清华学长分享自己的写作秘密，四十位高考作文学霸的走心经验谈。
《爱追剧？那你的作文有救了》	郭建华	即将出版	适读年龄：12～18岁。电视剧里有门道，藏着作文高分的小秘密。换个角度看电视，既追了剧，又写了作文。